Journey To The Heart Of God

Mystical Keys to Immortal Mastery

Almine

An Extraordinary Guide to Transfiguration

Published by Spiritual Journeys LLC

First Edition August 1, 2005

Copyright 2005

By Almine
Spiritual Journeys LLC
P.O. Box 300
Newport, Oregon 97365

Cover Illustration–Charles Frizzell

Text Design and Illustrations–Stacey Freibert

Manufactured in the United States of America

ISBN 0-9724331-2-0

Disclaimer

Please note that *Journey to the Heart of God: Mystical Keys to Immortal Mastery* is a documentary and reflects the personal experiences of Almine. This book is not to be interpreted as an independent guide to self-healing. Almine is not a doctor and does not practice medicine, and any information provided in this book should not be in lieu of consultation with your physician or other health care provider. Any reference to the word "Healer" refers to the individual healing experience that a client may have had. Any reference to Almine as a "Healer" is not to be interpreted that she is a certified medical professional, or that she practices medicine in any way. The word "Healer" only appears as a descriptive term used for Almine, as she merely acts as a guide for each client as they work through their own individual healing experience. Almine, Spiritual Journeys, or anyone associated with this book assumes no responsibility for the results of the use of any technique described in this book.

Table of Contents

Acknowledgements

I acknowledge with gratitude the invaluable contribution of Hilda in helping to polish and hone this book to its final format: to Robin and Margie and Mary for their work in helping to type and edit. My gratitude also goes to Therese and Dave for being part of our light family and bringing love and joy to my little girl's life. Thank you, Stacey, for the great illustrations and Charles Frizzell for the magic of his cover art.

With love,
Almine

Dedication

This book is dedicated to my little girl, Jaylene. Thank you, precious one, for the love and purity I see in your lovely little face and the fun we have together. Every day of my life is dedicated to making the world a better place for you and all children everywhere.

Preface

After three months of intense physical preparation in January 2004, Almine experienced a transfiguration, entering the presence of the Infinite for the second time since moving into God-consciousness (the state of no longer identifying with the ego) in 2000. In the weeks that followed, the powerful revelations contained in this book emerged from that all-encompassing silence.

Having lost most of her linear thinking during this transition, much of this book has been written without conscious thought. This form of automatic writing, like the automatic speaking she now does, flows freely from Source into her own handwriting from which it was transcribed.

Few who have entered into God-consciousness leave the bliss to teach. Still fewer enter the stage of Immortal Master and in addition continue to function among the masses; but as a Toltec nagual and seer, Almine's life is dedicated to leading others to complete freedom from mortal boundaries.

It is an opportunity of a lifetime to see through the eyes of one who has encountered the indescribable realms of eternity. From such a perspective come insights that can heal the deepest wounds of alienation found in human hearts. These sacred messages contain the true identity of mankind as light beacons of Creation and way-showers back to the heart of God.

Within this book some of the mysteries of the cosmos that have plagued seers for eons have been solved for the first time. Never before in the history of any mystery schools have such illuminating revelations challenged everything we thought we knew about the destiny of man. Within every fiber of our beings and in the depth of our hearts truth, no matter how profound, can be recognized for what it is, and it is truth that shall set us free.

Foreword

The way-showers of the world are my mission and my inspiration. My life is dedicated to you, the capstone of humanity. You are the ones who are not afraid to lay down old belief systems and open to the inpouring of Spirit.

We have come through time and space together, from the first moments of created life to meet upon this planet to turn the keys that will begin the journey home, back to the heart of God. I have been called forth for the specific task of touching the hearts of those who are the pillars of the temple, who uphold humanity by the light of their presence both now and in the future.

It is to you that I dedicate the teachings in this book. May your hearts recognize the many levels of light it imparts. May you and I pull forth even more light in the future so we may fill the earth with hope and peace and lay the path to a new tomorrow.

PART ONE

Journey To The
Heart God

THE LEAP TO FREEDOM

In order to reveal the many miracles that have produced the holy teachings contained within this book, it is necessary to recap some events that led up to my entry into God-consciousness.

In *A Life of Miracles, Mystical Keys to Ascension*, I wrote:

During the first week of November, 2000 I began to experience increased ecstatic states. The walls of my house were sometimes visible, sometimes not. Speaking had become almost redundant and everyone's intentions seemed crystal clear to me and their words were heard before they were said. I left on the first Friday of November for Dallas/Ft. Worth, Texas to teach a group of novices that had become familiar with my work through a beloved friend. ...Later that evening, as I gave my introductory talk, the Archangel Michael entered the class and channeled through me. He called himself Mi-ka-el and told the class members to ask for what they wanted and they would receive it. Many of them asked for expanded vision, to be able to see into the hidden realms, and because of this request they were able to see the great Masters of Light during the following two days as events unfolded.

At the end of the Friday night session, one woman was crying uncontrollably and relayed the following story: As she had set up the room in preparation for the event, she had been promised help from a few staff members of the hotel. Although they never came, a young man appeared and looked around as though he hadn't been there before. He said that he had come to help. His behavior was strange to her. He simply didn't seem like a hotel staff member and when he walked over to the table where she had displayed my tapes, he said, "She looks like an angel. This is going to be a very special event and they will need special water." He removed the tap water that had been set out in pitchers and came back with other water, saying, "This is special water for such a special event." After helping her set up the chairs he turned at the door and said over his shoulder, "Tell her my name is Mi-ka-el."

The next day the Master, Jesus Christ, appeared next to me, visible to many in class, and then moved into the space where I stood. I started to speak the words that I could hear within my head as He gave the prophecy, "Upon the backs of a few the future will pivot and great are the events of this holy day."

In the blink of an eye I lost all identity and disconnected from ego or body identification. ...At that moment I knew without a doubt that "IAM the I AM", meaning I am both the creation and the creator–the beginning and the end.

I was instructed not to let anyone touch me during that holy Saturday. ...My awareness had expanded to include all of creation and it seemed like a super-human task to walk or speak.

Any food or water sent me into a state of ecstasy. That night as I sat down to eat my dinner, a bite of salmon catapulted me into the entire life scenario of the fish I was eating. I saw him enthusi-

astically make his way down the river to the ocean. I felt the sting-ing of the salt in his gills for the first few days. I saw him rise to the surface of the ocean and through his eyes the sunset appeared yellowish-gold. I felt his fear as he struggled in the net and gasped his final breaths. Similarly I experienced the life of the grain and vegetables upon my plate.

The following day the experience continued. I felt myself observing my body from afar and at times I couldn't find it at all. In my lunch hour, when left alone, I felt as though I might vibrate out of this reality altogether. It was a struggle to stay in the physi-cal body. By the end of that day I embraced every one of the class members and tears just flowed. The holiness was so powerful there were no words for our feelings. By the evening when I left for the airport I wandered as though in a daze and had great difficulty being self-aware enough to become oriented to my environment.

Channelings came through one of my students during the com-ing days to give me instructions as to how to handle the God-real-ization into which I had been catapulted. Even language that was separation-based no longer fit into my comprehension. ...I was instructed to eat only that which 'lives' for energies would be entering my body that weren't from this universe. I did as instruct-ed but the words were meaningless to me, as all universes existed within me. Ecstatic states continued to be produced by the intake of any food or water.

An indescribable compassion poured forth from me that embraced every creature. Life was forever altered for me. I mir-rored the words from the Odes of Solomon, "Nothing appeared closed to me because I was the door of everything."

November 2000

For days after my entry into God-consciousness, I seemed to be in a state of shock. Layers of blankets couldn't warm the feeling of being chilled to the bone. Linear time seemed incomprehensible to me, instead time lay like a spider web around me, the possible futures as accessible as the past.

My physical energy was very low. I eliminated all unnecessary action in the physical world as I used my energy to explore the vastness within. Even things like getting the groceries seemed too much effort. I cancelled the main speaking engagements for the rest of the month. I ate only a diet of lightly cooked vegetables, fruit and water, as instructed. The purpose of this remained a mystery to me. I had lost all self-identity, all I knew was that I was nothing. At the time, even self-awareness seemed barely there and I clung to it for dear life. Losing self-identity was part of the experience; losing self-awareness, however, would plunge me into insanity. I seemed to have lost both short term and long term memory. When I tried to think of my childhood it seemed like a blank screen. Somehow, however, I could recall what I needed to when it was essential in making a decision.

The first major speaking engagement I agreed to was in December in Virginia. Moving my luggage and walking even short distances seemed too energy-consuming and I had to be helped as I walked to and from the car. Standing before the class the next morning, my thoughts and feelings seemed swallowed by the vastness within and material objects seemed to pulse with light. At times I could see through the walls of the room. I struggled to stay coherent for two hours until nausea overwhelmed me and I had to excuse myself and go to another room to lie down. Immediately I felt myself transported to a place I had been once before when I levitated before a group of male students assembled in my house. As before, I stood next to Jesus Christ above the world. He told me that my prayers to ease the sufferings of the children of the planet had been heard. I had offered my very identity as an individuated being in exchange for alleviation of their pain and I had been heard. Christ said that the personality–'the soul piece'–that was in my body would leave the cosmos to merge back into the heart of God. One of my light bodies was to take the place of the personality that would leave. It would be done so that the mission of the former personality piece could continue in physicality. Although I knew that our light bodies are stacked inside each other like Russian dolls, occupying larger and larger areas of space until eventually the highest light body fills the entire cosmos, I was still not familiar enough with them to know which one to choose. I knew that when beings of very high frequency enter physicality, the consciousness of every living being on earth is raised.

Taking this into consideration, I chose the highest light body that could still retain physical form. It came from another universe and within a few minutes the transfer was completed. The former individuated personality moved out of the body altogether and the high light body walked in. The previous personality left the cosmos, merging back into the Infinite on April 12, 2005–something that had never been done before.

I was barely able to function during the rest of that day. It felt as though I had concussion. Linear time was a strange concept to me. Images of events that would take place together with the steps I would take to accomplish them appeared.

Information about an occurrence of great importance that would take place on a hill in Virginia was given to me. That evening at dusk some of my students dropped me off at the bottom of the hill. Alone, on wobbly legs, I carefully climbed to the top. I sat down to wait. Immediately after, a potent wave of power shook my body. The next instant a portal between realms opened and I saw Lucifer standing before the multitudes of darkness. Information flooded my being. I saw how the voluntary descent into forgetfulness that one-third of the host of heaven made under the leadership of Lucifer, enabled creation to occur.

As one-third of the sons and daughters of Light dimmed their light, the cosmos was pulled into the lower realm of existence where materialization could take place. I saw the tremendous inclusive compassion that precipitated the act of sacrifice of Lucifer and his hosts. They were the nobility, the bravest of the brave, to believe so much that the evolution of awareness needed to take place that they agreed to forgo feeling joy and love for eons of time so that polarity could exist.

Without one-third of us embodying the chaos, there would be no movement and evolution of God's awareness. The contribution made by Lucifer and his hosts was epic in scope and it was done trusting that we would one day remember our oneness and in doing so, take them along as we returned to the heart of God.

I stood up to honor the role of those playing the undeveloped light and as I did so, a portal beyond them unlocked. They walked through and although still contained within their own realm, a flicker of remembrance of their origins of light returned.

I returned to Oregon, having newly walked into the human form and resumed the life of the former Almine. Although I entered into her relationships and shared many of her skills and knowledge, there were some blatant differences. She knew how to dress well and I did not. She had remained young and after I entered, the body started to age. The previous personality was vivacious and talked with humor, whereas I seldom laughed. She had been light on her feet, I felt clumsy and the body felt like a heavy lump of clay.

It took many months to properly communicate with my classes in an understandable way. Words seemed inadequate, in fact ridiculous, to convey the profound revelations I was receiving.

A Vessel of Divine Compassion

God-consciousness requires one to adjust. For example, information does not imprint. I needed notes in order to remember whether or not I had brushed my teeth. There was simply no future and no past. This was compounded by the fact that memory is kept in electromagnetic fields and these fields are very low around a being in God-consciousness.

I felt emptied out of emotion except for a vast loneliness. I knew without a shadow of a doubt that there was no being besides myself in the entire cosmos. I was no-thing, empty and alone. I sat wrapped in blankets, hardly moving for days.

I alternated between expansion and contraction. One moment I felt the entire cosmos within, then the terror that I might lose contact with my body plummeted my awareness back into a contracted state. The claustrophobia of being back in the confines of the body would then cause me to go into hyperventilation.

2001

The terror accompanying these alternating states of expansion and contraction remained throughout the first three months of the year. The feeling of being chilled to the bone continued into late April. It was virtually impossible to make a decision since I had lost all personal desire.

At the beginning of September, I had to speak at an Indigenous conference in Wilsonville, Oregon. But the night before, horrible dreams of death and carnage disturbed my sleep. The experience had been so real. I felt nauseated, my body shaking. I made my way to class and tried to lecture, but was badly shaken. The video taping of the class had already begun, but I could only stammer, "I'm sorry, but I need a chair and some water. I feel terribly weak. I've been in the cockpit with crazed Middle Eastern men who flew planes into buildings."

I was quite sure my class thought I was entirely insane, but two days later 9/11 occurred in the United States.

Encountering the Bliss

Moving to the outer edges of the vast inner map that stretched across the cosmos like a spider web, I could slip into a velvety silence. There I was fully expanded and functioning from my highest self. It was a tremendous energy drain when I had to contract in order to relate to another.

After having been in the state of emptiness for close to a year, I started feeling a new frequency in the cells of my body. It felt like rippling laughter; as though I could disintegrate into a puddle of bliss. Objects seemed to move through me and others felt as though they were within me. Spirals of light emitting from objects joined with my own in one beautiful vibrating field. The thoughts and feelings of others felt like my own. This was very different from the way I had experienced the thoughts and feelings of others during my classes when I had been in expanded states, but still in identity consciousness. I could access the feelings then, but they felt separate from myself. Now everyone I met seemed part of me.

When lecturing, I asked to be left alone during breaks so that I could disappear into the bliss until the class pulled me back. The bliss was intoxicating. It was like sensations induced by morphine, which I had been given while in the hospital for the birth of one of my children.

Bliss is one of the greatest temptations seers face and it can halt growth. Looking back, I can see that during this period of emptiness and then fullness, my growth was less than at any other time in my life. Why this phase traps most mystics from progressing further became very clear. It felt like the most wonderful place imaginable.

Immersed in bliss, I remained highly disoriented. To the amusement of my audiences, I often couldn't find the door or my car or even the steps to the podium. In Portland, Oregon I crawled onto the stage on my hands and knees and once more my audience thought I must be mad. I performed tasks as though on auto-pilot. Raising my voice was very unpleasant–my senses were so heightened it sounded like thunder in my ears. There was no impulse to laugh aloud as laughter was occurring all the time within. I saw the folly of others, but the focus of this stage was mostly on the perfection of the big picture.

2002

At the beginning of the year I started to see flashes of dynamic, moving geometry but I couldn't "connect the dots". While leading a week-long workshop with sixteen women at my home, I asked for their assistance. I had them lie in a circle around me on the back lawn, feet towards the center where I stood. They directed energy at a crystal I held in my hand. The energy they produced was so strong it burnt a circle where I had stood that remained for months.

Shaken by the experience, I staggered to bed. A little sphere of light appeared in front of me and entered my forehead. I was pulled out of my body and found myself standing within a multi-faceted polyhedron. Another was rotating within and a diffuse field was forming between the inner and outer polyhedrons. Light bounced between the field and the outer polyhedron. The shapes of Platonic solids seemed to appear within the pattern of dancing light. I heard the words, "No angles and no joints".

Soon after, I went to England and a dear friend brought someone to meet me. She intuitively knew this meeting was meant to be. Her guest had become an expert in dynamic geometry after receiving it in a near-death experience and provided the mathematical terminology for the images I had seen.

That night I received another vision with clearer images and was told again that our belief that geometry had angles and joints was part of the illusion of this density. The geometry of creation lived and breathed, pulsed and replicated itself. In the morning when I awoke, I was levitating above the bed with my right foot in my left hand and my left foot in my right hand. My limbs were carefully arranged so as not to touch. Once again I heard the words, "No angles and no joints", loudly and clearly. Two years later this information would help me unlock one of the secrets of the universe seers had tried to solve for eons.

Pods of Light

When someone enters God-consciousness, the shock of making contact with the Infinite causes wear and tear on the emotional body. The emotional body is responsible for relaying energy from the higher bodies to the physical and when disrupted, lowered energy levels are experienced. I was still struggling with lowered energy during most of the year but I began training my first small groups of apprentices.

The great master Melchizedek, who often gives me messages through a dear friend and unconscious channel, called them 'Pods'. He sent me the message that it was about time I finally understood that this was my task. The Pods were dedicated to self-work. During a week in August one of the women's Pods in my home had an extraordinary experience and the rational minds of some of the women were so loosened that they entered into God-consciousness. Part of the amazing experiences included being taken aboard an Andromedan craft and shown how to work with timelines. This was done to show us so how to move the planet out of the way of potential catastrophes that lay in its future. We spent many hours out of body each day doing work on several continents and the planet herself. We were warned that from the work we had done, a very noticeable time-space anomaly would occur the following day within a twenty-mile radius of my house.

Later that day, after we had worked with the timelines, a former NASA scientist and Pleidian contactee called to say the Andromedans had contacted him and he was to tell me that impending damage to the earth had been averted due to a shift of its timeline. He added that a large part of national dharma (collective karma) had been cleared in the Middle East.

The time-space anomaly became apparent the next day when my office manager, unaware of what we had done, drove to work from out of town. She came into the office, with a bewildered look; "It's the strangest thing. About twenty miles from here it felt as though I was entering into another reality. It almost felt as though I was driving into a gelatinous substance."

I had to go to my bank and for the first time ever, found a line of customers trailing out onto the sidewalk. I decided to go to another branch, only to discover the same strange sight. The bank clerks were so confused that it took them four hours to notarize fifteen pages of paperwork. The branch clerk called my primary bank for information and the response was, "I'm sorry, my head aches. I can't think straight. I can't possibly deal with this today."

Driving around town, people seemed to be in a dazed state. Several times I had to evade cars whose drivers seemed oblivious to my presence.

Two Andromedans, a male and a female, appeared and lingered around me for another six months, providing additional information especially when I was lecturing. When I would place my index finger on my third eye, the tall bluish beings would appear, one either side of me, to give the information I needed.

No Point of Arrival

Through the intoxication of the bliss, I would often hear the words, "There is no point of arrival. Live where the straight and the curved lines meet." Continuing to function as though in a dream and, when left to my own devices, disappearing into the fullness of the bliss, these words became more insistent. I understood what it meant to live where the curved and straight lines meet for I had seen in visions that the straight lines are the movement of the form of awareness most dominant during God-consciousness and the curved lines were part of the form of awareness that was most prevalent during separation consciousness. What the words were telling me was that I had to re-enter the human condition while remembering that I was all things. No sooner had I made that decision, than I moved to the next phase of God-consciousness; re-entry into the human condition. Once again it happened in an instant.

A Pod sister and I were playing Schubert's Military Waltz as a duet on the piano in my home. She was playing the upper part much more expertly than I was playing the bass. After two years of having scarcely any childhood memories, I spontaneously recalled having played the same duet in the same way with a school friend when I was twelve. We had played in the Cape Town

City Hall, performing it beautifully except for the last four chords, which turned into an inharmonious mess. The look on my friend's face as she glanced at me in despair, struck me as so funny that I broke out laughing in front of the audience. Remembering, I broke out laughing once again.

When the sister and I completed the piece, I staggered to a chair–something felt entirely different. My memories had returned and with them, emotions. I could now fully participate in life while remembering it is just a game.

Once more I started to notice my body. During the past two years I had aged more than in the fifty years preceding my entry into God-consciousness. I had felt hardly any emotions and it was as though the body's metabolism had slowed down. While playing the duet I had re-entered the human experience and a new interest in life took hold of me. I again felt passion for exploring earth and its many hidden treasures. The joys of simple things were restored.

Receiving the Sacred Symbols

One night in prayer (prayer is entirely different when one knows there is no being outside of oneself in all the cosmos), I used the names of the seven Lords of Light that guard and govern the seven levels of light on earth. They are located in the Halls of Amenti within the earth and I had been brought before them on another occasion. As I called their names, symbols about a foot in height appeared in front of my face. I wished for a pen and paper but did not want to disturb the communication. I continued to call their names and the symbols kept appearing. When I had finished, I was very disappointed that I could not retain them.

The next morning I decided to try again and sat with pen and paper while calling upon the Lords of Light. To my joy, the symbols once again appeared. I drew them as carefully as I could, but I

15

noticed that if even one angle or line was slightly incorrect the symbol would linger until it was corrected. The relationship between the lines and angles seemed to be critically important. Not only was I given the seven symbols for the lords, but also one for the Dweller–the great Master who guards the stability of the planetary axis and the future unfoldment of life on earth.

When I gave these sacred symbols to the Pod sisters, one of them felt the need to have the symbol of the Dweller (also called Horlet) drawn at the base of her spine, and enlisted the help of a friend. Later that day we went to pray at a sacred site where many women's groups had gone before. Walking ahead of the others along the path, I heard a commotion behind me. I turned to see the sister who had used the symbol collapsed on the ground. Running to her, I laid my jacket under her head, noticing that her breath was becoming still and her spirit was beginning to leave her body. She was dying. I called her spirit back into the body and blew energy into the area of her womb. After several minutes of not breathing, she gasped for air and life returned to her eyes. Although very shaken, she bravely made her way to the sacred site and we proceeded with our prayers for the planet.

When we returned to my home, her spirit again wanted to leave. This time I not only saw the spirit leaving, but saw an incredible being of light attempting to enter. We were experiencing a walk-in situation as had happened in my own life. We stood around her to help her make her transition and prepare her body to receive the great light that would enter. The majesty and glory that shot forth as the high being entered, left us speechless. Through very hard work, she had prepared her body that year to accommodate such a light by removing all filters that could obstruct it.

I was concerned about her ability to travel home, yet she assured me everything would be fine. At the airport she saw an old acquaintance who said she had been training with a Toltec teacher, author of a very popular book and a well-known name in Hollywood. She said she had studied with him two weeks every other month for years. The sister was amazed; "How do you do it? We only go to Almine every other month and it is so intense we can barely stand it!" The acquaintance replied, "Oh, we have a lot of fun! It isn't difficult at all." The sister was confused. Fun? Perhaps she had gotten the wrong teacher, for she had cried so much that year that she felt as though she had no more tears to cry. She had embraced the pain of her past until she was able to release it as the insights were extracted.

Suddenly the acquaintance started to panic, obsessing about whether airport security would search her. She wanted to trade positions in line, claiming that they were checking every seventh person. The sister agreed but was now even more confused, "How could she have been training that long and that often and still be able to be upset by such petty things?" Her own agitation and clamor of mind had long since been left behind. It was then that she realized the gift of facing our pain: inner stillness.

When she returned home to her family, she was so completely different that she even changed her name to one more harmonious with the new frequency. Her clothes, hair, and the priorities of her life had completely changed.

The following month, while teaching a Pod, I went into an involuntary trance state and accessed the ancient Goddess symbols. These symbols represent the goddess archetypes studied in the mystery schools of the divine feminine. Many of these schools had been exterminated before they had had the chance to complete their purpose. I had seen that this particular POD had as its overall purpose (each POD seemed to have an unstated task to perform) completing the mission of the ancient female mystery schools.

Soon after, again in the trance state, the symbols of the god arche-types came as well. Later, when I compared them to the goddess symbols, I saw how beautifully they fitted together. I could feel the power of these symbols as keys to entire bodies of information representing cosmic principals that apply to all Creation. Their holiness is unmistakable.

In December, I received a gift from the great master, Merlin. Unlike the gift from Sunat Kumara and the object given to me by Thoth that awakened the ancient languages (see *A Life of Miracles*), this gift remained in the fourth dimension. It was called the Seer's Stone and could be seen only when in altered states. With it came the prophecy that in the forthcoming year I would solve the mystery of human DNA. The stone played a major part in that discovery. Hanging on a chain around my neck, it was in the middle of a ring of twelve diamonds of the purest colors repre-senting the twelve strands of the human DNA. The Seer's Stone in the center is really a passageway or portal. The same principle applies in human DNA where this portal is the key to our passage back to the heart of God. The stone increased the rate at which my thoughts would manifest.

2003

A Message From Pan

In January, dreams of great destruction plagued my sleep with visions of starvation, plague, warfare and a comet hitting the earth. A great sadness settled upon me. The least favorite part of my teaching has always been prophecy, yet I felt responsible for those who depended on me for guidance.

In March, I taught in Toronto–exactly in the middle of the SARS outbreak. The level of fear was very high and my telling about these visions would only add to the consternation. I decided at first to say nothing.

One of the participants in class is a natural seer and can see energy directly as though solid, a completely different way than seeing clairvoyantly on the screen of the mind. This sister had lived all her life in God-consciousness and carefully conceals the incredible reality that is her day-to-day life. During class I noticed her watching all the beings that I could only sense in the room. Suddenly her expression went from amazement to repressed amusement as she stared directly at something in the middle of the room. Finally she interrupted, "Do you folks realize that Pan, the nature god, is dancing up a storm in the middle of our circle, trying to get our attention? He has been hovering around here for two weeks, waiting for Almine to arrive. Now he just has to speak."

We had a brief recess and I went upstairs with her and Pan so that she could interpret his words to me. He was aware that the currently configured future would bring huge devastation and nuclear contamination. His concern was the large comet heading toward the earth. In my visions, I had seen the great loss of life it would bring. Pan asked that I do something to deflect this terrible future. Before leaving, he said he would return to confirm that it had been done.

I decided to discuss the prophecies with the class, all of whom could hardly contain their curiosity over Pan's visit. I tried to instill hope in them as I spoke of the predictions. Pan wouldn't have asked us for assistance if he didn't feel that we could prevent these events. I felt somehow the answer lay in my ability to work with timelines through the instructions given the previous year by the Andromedans.

In August a women's group arrived at my house. After preparations, we gathered at a sacred site and applied the methods provided by the Andromedans on pivoting the timelines through our hearts. Somehow it didn't feel quite complete, as though it had turned but not locked into place.

I wrote the following in my journal: <u>3rd thru the 10th of August, 2003, Oregon Coast:</u> *Twenty women arrive and I become aware that each one has been carefully selected by Spirit for their purity. Past experience warns not to leave tracks that can be traced by the undeveloped light. Therefore, I have set aside thoughts of the forthcoming task and have quieted my mind. We will have to be ready at a moment's notice to do as Spirit instructs. I feel the support of thousands of Lightworkers who are lending their prayers to assist us with this work. During the week as we merge into group consciousness, the power escalates. We are instructed on August 10 to pivot the earth's timeline into an altered reality. We are to go to a location on the beach where several previous groups have dedicated their lives and prayers to the planet over the past six years. There we will apply the techniques given by the Andromedans.*

<u>11th of August, 2003:</u> *Before these holy women leave my home, I warn them that the events of yesterday are not to be analyzed or even contemplated. Although it feels incomplete, I know the cosmos will confirm when we have succeeded*

<u>12th of August, 2003:</u> *I am aware this day holds significance for healing the rift in our time-space continuum, but I ignore it. One woman remains as she wishes to take some inter-dimensional photographs of me and my home, a rare gift she possesses. My guest asks if she can photograph me in prayer before the altar in my sacred room. I agree. What happens next comes as a huge surprise. Suddenly, we find ourselves in a portal where space seems liquid and thousands of people, who had been trapped by time-travel experiments, walk free and step into this new timeline. A*

blue-light explosion seems to click the previously incomplete rotation of the timeline into place. The intensity of it shocks our cells and we find ourselves virtually unable to walk. At that moment, the task is complete. We are no longer in the direct path of the huge rocks hurtling through space. Although the comet is still coming in this new timeline, an indentation has formed in the time-space continuum and when it hits that indentation, it will veer off course and miss the earth. The future will be gentler now.

The Power of Emotion

As the year wore on, strange emotions arose within me. Re-entering the human condition, I had felt the full range of emotions, but only superficially, like the surface of the ocean in a storm while the depths are still. Now, however, the emotions seemed strong enough to affect my equilibrium. I felt off-balance, needy, thoroughly bewildered and ashamed that at this advanced stage of awareness such a thing could occur. How could I regress to such a level? For a long time, desires had really only been preferences.

For many years, love for everyone had become impersonal, simply flowing through me, flooding anything I focused on. I was like an actor staying in character on stage, yet remembering it was just a play. Neediness had been left behind many years ago. Suddenly it reared its ugly head again. I began developing an obsessive desire for a family group around me. I wished that a few of the Pod students would form a 'family' even though I knew without a doubt that in order to lead others to freedom the seer must have no agendas with his or her students.

I stayed in eagle vision, objectively watching this strange desire that far exceeded just a preference. It was growing into a bewildering need. Where could such neediness originate when I could in an instant enter into a vastness where I knew there was no creation separate from myself?

This dysfunctional need remained for nine months, growing stronger in intensity. I observed how my higher self deliberately sabotaged this need from being fulfilled. Every attempt I made to create a small group that could be my 'family' would somehow crumble. Although perplexed, I felt I should let it run its course. To suppress it would merely strengthen it. Perhaps there had been some tremendous lesson I had failed to learn.

One morning in October I awoke and said: "From this day on my body shall transform and expel all toxins and unwanted substances." Within one day, I had a burning fever and for the next three months chemicals, metals and other toxins poured out of my body. Even two baths a day didn't seem enough. Acidic smells came through the skin of the entire body. Fevers came and went for several weeks as viral or bacterial infections came to a head. Tormenting emotions and physical distress became so severe that I asked for a conversation with the master, Melchizedek. His answer was: "Almine is preparing for entry into the Null in the first weeks of January. She will then understand what this is about."

I tried to focus on my work with students where a fascinating revelation was emerging. In tracking patterns and cycles of challenges, we could map out themes linked to past lives. We traced them back as far as we could in an attempt to unravel their individual destinies–those contracts they had made with the Infinite as to what portion of the mystery of beingness they would solve.

To my great surprise, all the students' past lives led back in a loop to the future. A fascinating picture of the future and its destruction emerged. It was clear that we had designed this loop back in time to learn the lessons that would create a different future.

2004
The Transfiguration

In January I went into seclusion. On the 5th I had visionary experiences as powerful as those experienced during my entry into God-consciousness. The walls of my house became transparent, the experience growing until it encompassed all space and time. It turned into the vastness that Melchizedek had referred to as the 'Null'; the presence of the Infinite. For an incalculable amount of time I received vast bodies of information that seemed to be assimilated instantaneously.

I saw the destiny of humankind–the ultimate creation that carries the fate of the cosmos. I understood how the sub-personalities of humans were the key to the successful completion of the future and elimination of much unnecessary suffering. Overwhelming bliss flooded my being, which became borderless and vast.

Then came an experience that can only be described as 'falling out of heaven'. I felt myself plunging into a demonic darkness, terrifying beyond description. I had never experienced anything remotely like this oppressive darkness. The sheer weight of the blackness was suffocating and I yearned with all my heart to be free of it. Then as suddenly as it had come, the darkness receded, leaving behind crushing grief.

The darkness was the darkness of the unknown portions of the Infinite's being. Since I was all things, this darkness was also mine. When it left, it felt as though a piece of me was being torn away and a great sense of loss and agony overwhelmed me. Now I understood the need for the Infinite to reclaim its unknown pieces. I realized that the Christ had undergone a similar event in the Garden of Gethsemane. Something within me shattered. I lay in a state of shock, trembling and cold, hugging my knees in a fetal position. For what seemed like hours, I tried to make sense of the pain and loss I still felt. I could see that that which had shattered was the fields around my body–they had split into three parts.

I had known for some time the work I was doing was that of a nagual, or Toltec seer whose reason for existence is to lead others to freedom. My approach, however, was so unique that I hesitated to call myself a nagual. I had extreme caution in giving myself any labels since labels trap our growth. It became crystal clear during this transfiguration that I am a three-pronged nagual whose destiny is and always has been to lead others to freedom from illusion. I could see why my Toltec training had come through telepathy: I wouldn't be told what seers could or couldn't know; I would, as a result, solve mysteries that had eluded Toltec seers for eons.

Now I could see the purpose of the preceding months of seeming insanity: the emotional fields around the body spin clockwise and the mental fields spin counter-clockwise (called the Merkaba). When a strong emotion becomes an obsession and is contrary to the level of perception, it sets up a vortex within the luminous cocoon (the cocoon is the seven bodies of man, ranging from the physical to the spirit body, stacked within each other like Russian dolls) that cracks it, thereby transfiguring the fields. As suddenly as it had emerged, the obsessiveness disappeared.

Life changed dramatically after this transfiguration. I was catapulted into the third and final stage of the evolution of man's awareness, that of the Ascended Master. My tears flowed frequently during the first three months of 2004 as compassion moved me deeply. It was impossible to look at a flower, a hawk circling above or the beautiful face of a child without crying for joy. I did not understand that the silent flooding of love was the result of the now complete mental silence, until I was shown in a dream.

The silence within my mind before the transfiguration was there virtually all the time, but I had to leave the silence when relating to another or analyzing or deducing a course of action. The silence now became all-encompassing, swallowing every thought and emotion, even when lecturing or writing. In the silence of the mind, the heart could fully open.

In this new stage many changes occurred. The physical purification had stopped overnight. If I allowed too long a gap between sentences, I would be encompassed by the silence and forget that I was speaking at all. As a result, I spoke rapidly so that I would not get lost in the silence. It was impossible to undertake any action not in accordance with the blueprint of my life as designed by my higher self. If I tried to leave the house when I wasn't supposed to, I could not raise my hand to open the door. Any resistance to life produced the sensation of being in a vortex of swirling energy. After a week of training two Canadian sisters, they asked me out to dinner. I wanted to accept but couldn't make my mouth say, "Yes". I finally had to say, "I don't know why, but I'm unable to say 'Yes'." As it turned out, the two of them had incredibly visionary experiences on the beach that they were able to capture on film. I was delayed in traffic for two hours. If I had said, 'Yes', they would have had to interrupt their beautiful experience and wait for me in vain.

In the previous stage of God-consciousness, I could see in all directions, possible futures as well as the past. Now all I could see clearly was my next step. Before going to bed one night, I wondered how best to surrender to this new stage of development. I dreamt that the ceiling of my house was leaking and the rain was breaking it down more and more. Immediately before waking, I said to myself, "I must have the ceiling repaired", but I heard the answer: "Just allow the process of life to break down your previous limitations".

In another dream I was standing in front of an audience in India. The moderator hadn't introduced me to the audience, so the students looked at me blankly, not knowing who I was. It didn't bother me. These were highly evolved students, I thought, surely they would recognize how sacred the truths were that I was sharing. But they were paying very little attention to me. Suddenly, they all fell in reverence to their knees. "Oh, wonderful! They can see the sacredness of what I have just said," I thought. But then I noticed a yogi on a stretcher being carried through the back of the room and realized they were kneeling to him. "What's going on?" I asked, amazed. The moderator responded, "Don't you know who that is? That is Yogi such-and-such!" As I woke up, I could hear a voice: "You have no identify. But you are speaking to those who do, so it is necessary for you to describe the role you play as a teacher". I called my staff and the next morning my role of nagual was listed on my website.

The Goddess Reveals Herself

After the transfiguration I no longer had expectations regarding my students, even those who over the years had become as close as my family. What they chose to do no longer concerned me when confronted with life-altering choices. All that mattered was that I kept my part of providing them with the highest guidance.

After losing the same pair of gloves three times, I understood that the gloves had to come off with my students. My commitment now only supported indwelling life. I was no longer able to tolerate the slightest dishonesty they may have had with themselves. My style appeared tougher, even though I had moved into a place of greater love. Insights that previously would have taken me hours to puzzle out, were now instantly there. No thinking was necessary. I traveled easily and deeply into the realms of un-manifested life and had as much energy at my disposal as needed.

At the end of January, I solved a secret that had puzzled seers for over a million years of oral history. The Infinite and Creation consist of four great bands of compassion, two within Creation and the previously unsolved two that lay within the Infinite. These four frequency bands are the matrix of creation and are mirrored everywhere just like, for instance, the Fibonaci sequence. Once I had solved the nature of the frequency bands, I could see how all life follows this pattern. That which grows through stages of maturation and resolution, including our emotional and social development, sexual stages, conflict resolution–all follow this eternal pattern. By aligning ourselves with this matrix, we would be aligning with the power of the Infinite and its Creation.

I had been unaware of a riddle, unsolved by seers throughout Toltec history until my visionary experiences on January 5. It was communicated to me that the ascended masters of this planet have always told seers that if the mysterious relationship between the three and the four (represented by the three-pronged and four-pronged naguals) could be solved by one in human form, life would make a huge evolutionary leap in consciousness. Not having had a physical teacher, I only became aware of it as part of the body of information I received during my mystical experiences.

It seemed imperative that it be solved by someone within physicality, or else the information would have simply been given. In 2002 when I received the dynamic geometry, I had been told it was in preparation for solving the great mystery. Perhaps this relationship between the Three and the Four was the mystery that was meant.

On May 30, a new Women's Pod arrived for their second week of instruction. From the moment those seven light-filled women arrived, I felt something huge was about to happen. The first day, a sister from Curacao explained she had been sent by Catholic saints who told her I would be able to assist them in reversing the actions of black magicians. She said a great deal of dark and destructive sorcery was regularly done by those who practice in South and Central America. Their black sorcery was usually done in the name of the various saints. She had promised to bring a resolution to this situation and was told that I held the key.

Following a series of events, I became aware that I held judgment against practitioners who use the powers of the hidden realms to injure or bind others with dark arts. Their unscrupulous practices and lack of perception damage the web of life. This causes an imbalance in nature and has, on several occasions, resulted in great cataclysms to the planet that have caused the fall in consciousness of man. I knew humankind had to descend in order to be able to ascend, but still had a negative emotional response to black magic.

During the first two days of training this Pod, I traveled out of body during lunch breaks to see from an eagle's perspective why my vision surrounding this topic was limited. I saw the numerals '999' and then a crystal was placed between myself and the numerals. They now appeared as '666'. What this symbolized was that deep inside we all know we should be able to make a profound difference to our fellow man through every choice we make. When the knowledge of how to do this in a positive way becomes obscured, we seem disempowered and the ability to impact negatively seems preferable to having no ability at all. In many of the countries where large numbers of black magicians lived, life is reduced to survival. In such hopelessness there is very little thought given to the long term consequences of such actions.

By the third morning I could embrace with compassion this area where previously there had been judgment. As the Pod and I sat down for opening prayers, I heard clearly, "This is the day for the key to be turned. This is the day the planet will move up an overtone." I shared the message with the sisters that someone would turn a key that day. I asked them to feel the frequency of the trees and the earth, for later it would sing a different song due to the upward shift in frequency.

Right before lunch, to my own amazement, I uttered these words, "I will be traveling out of body during the break to solve the mystery between the three and the four." My feet automatically took me to the kitchen where I had a calendar picturing crop glyphs photographed in England during 2003. I barely had had time to glance at it, when I found myself turning to a page showing three crop glyphs that had appeared in the same location over a two-year period.

Through the knowledge of dynamic geometry, I could see that these images weren't depicting our third-dimensional, illusion-based geometry with its angles and joints. The crop glyphs clearly indicated that the four sprang from the three; the square was created from a triangle and it represented the relationship between the three higher bodies and four lower bodies. A stigmata manifested on my left leg in the middle of my shin. It was the exact replica of one of the crop glyphs I was contemplating.

During my out of body experience, it became crystal clear that the Infinite and its Creation, comprised of the four great frequency bands of compassion, were the mental, emotional, etheric (astral) and physical bodies of a vast being of indescribable consciousness. Beyond it lay three additional frequencies; the spiritual-emotional, the spiritual-mental and spirit body of this vast being in whom we reside.

A being in identity consciousness tries to function using only its four lower bodies to run its life. The mental body keeps its hold on the being's life by blocking information from the three higher bodies; in other words, it forms a barrier. A being that enters into God-consciousness removes this barrier of the mental body so that the three higher bodies become the operators of that life.

To entities in higher realms these truths must be apparent. After all, they drew them in the crop glyphs of England. But all of Creation waited for understanding to dawn in the densest levels. It was in physicality that the key of perception had to unlock the barrier of the mental body and allow the influence of the three higher bodies to filter through. As I understood the relationship between the three and the four; square upon square unlocked to its creative triangle into what seemed like eternity (the square representing the four lower bodies, and the triangle representing the three higher bodies). Eventually I stood before the largest square, the four great bands of compassion. Another door opened and the new energy flooded into the densest levels of creation. The true Goddess, the Mother of all things, the three higher bodies that created the Infinite was filling all Creation with her love.

When I returned to the body, I was in poor condition. My breathing was shallow and I could hardly walk. I explained to the sisters what had occurred and the enormity of it left us speechless. We listened to Handel's "Messiah" while attempting to internalize these extraordinary insights by understanding them within our hearts. Above the house, the heavens opened and I could see a column of angels descending. They blew on trumpet-like instruments. The frequency raised the earth to the next over-tone.

My condition grew worse by the hour. The cells in my body were on fire and felt as though they would burst with the energy they contained. I was trembling and by early evening, waves of tremendous terror and pain hit me in the solar plexus. To the best of my ability, amidst waves of nausea, I could only make out that the grids around the planet were releasing the fear and anguish that had been programmed into them. I was to become a filter to move it through me and convert it into light, but it wasn't moving through. During the out of body experience I had stood before the greatest gate of all and three great gatekeepers had guarded it; one light, one neutral and one dark. A dark being, huge and ominous, had followed me back and I now came under the worst attack I had ever endured.

The beloved sisters stood around my bed, but as the night wore on I started to seriously doubt whether I would survive. I had long since lost any food I had consumed that day and waves of pain and fear continued to bombard my solar plexus. I felt as if a spike had been driven into my head. Due to the trauma, the fields around my body had been bumped into a distorted configuration and I could feel my life force leaking out. In the early morning hours I asked the sisters to call my friend and unconscious channel and ask for guidance from Melchizedek. Minutes before the phone rang, he awoke to find a dark being entering into his bedroom from the study. He asked where the other two were, instantly aware that there should be three gatekeepers.

In my haze of pain and nausea I had failed to notice the distortion in my body's fields. I was struggling for every breath and was mentally saying goodbye to my children. Through the channeler's advice and the insight of one sister, I was able to move the octahedronal fields around my body back into position. This immediately reduced the pain by 50%. Together the sisters stood around my bed and banished the darkness. I felt the tide turn and knew everything would be fine. I was able to sleep for the remainder of that night, but was unable to teach the next morning. The headaches, where the spike had been driven into my head, lingered for several days and my full strength didn't return for two weeks.

It is said that when much is given, much is expected. But it is also true that when much is expected, much is given. My abilities increased once my strength came back. I now had enough energy to transport my body with me as I traveled into the future. It left in segments, like rings stacked together that fell over one at a time. When I arrived at my destination, my body re-assembled the same way. Once, I materialized in a locked room with four people present. Their startled and shocked looks made me laugh. When I returned, my body again came together in a series of rings or segments. Although I had spent days in the future, only 45 minutes had passed on the clock. My body felt refreshed and filled with energy.

Perhaps because of these incredible experiences we were privileged to share, during the third and final Pod class of the year this entire group of women went into God-consciousness in one afternoon. This miracle was their reward for the courage they exhibited and their willingness to stand by my side during what was for me the physical testing or crucifixion.

Venus Transit

On June 8, 2004 an astrological phenomenon known as a Venus transit occurred. It started on June 6, three days after my physical trial, when Venus moved across the face of the sun between the earth and the sun. The last Venus transit happened 121 years ago and because Venus transits come in pairs, the next one will occur in 8 years, minus two days. The next occurrence is marked exactly by the auspicious event of the end of the Mayan calendar.

Every Venus transit signals tremendous breakthroughs in communication and world views, such as Magellan's journey around the world to prove it was not flat, the instigation of the postal systems, or the emergence of the right of women to vote. Modern astrologers have heralded this 2004 transit as the 'Advent of the Divine Feminine'. Some astrologers have connected it to the goddess archetypes rising, claiming that the forthcoming years are a prime opportunity to re-connect with the feminine principle.

The event that occurred heralds the Creatress of the Infinite, the holy Mother of God, pouring her life-giving love into Creation; an event that will leave life as we know it forever altered. It means the end to poverty and disease in the near future and immortality to Creation during this creational cycle.

ALMINE

PART TWO

Mystical Keys to Immortal Mastery

SECRETS OF THE COSMOS

The Loop Of Time

Each time a universe has moved back into oneness from separation, the denser elements that would not transfigure back into light were repelled (with light and frequency <u>opposite</u> poles repel) into the void. This made it necessary to form another universe around these dense elements. Every time this happened, life was pushed into lower and lower octaves of Creation.

Our present wave-form universe has reached the end of time and space allotted to this creational cycle. There is no place to repel the density to and it cannot be taken over the edge on the in-breath or contraction back to the heart of God. We cannot leave behind any part of ourselves (the One expressing as the many) yet neither can we take the density back without resolving it.

The designers of this universe had to devise a solution to what appeared to be a stalemate: not only had the dense elements become more dense with each lowering of frequency, but they had accumulated, creating a 'bottom–heavy' universe.

Each time a universe had to be formed, light beings from the highest levels had to de-evolve to play roles opposite the ones in forgetfulness. They did this by assuming some of the dense energy. In this way, the expansion of Creation has been slowed by the dark (unyielded light) becoming less dark and the light less light. When the polarity between light and dark lessens, the rate of expansion slows; when the poles are farther apart in degree, expansion accelerates. More and more light workers have lost their way into forgetfulness as life has fallen octave by octave. The result is that the dark may be less dark, but there is more of it. In addition, we need momentum to propel us over the edge of the tube torus (a doughnut-shaped expansion of Creation turning outward and inward upon itself) and we are losing momentum.

The designers of the universe knew that the final solution to this seeming problem had to mirror the fourth band of compassion: unity within diversity (this is explained in a later chapter). A template had to be designed in which separate races would form a family of diversity; they would be sub-personalities of the whole.

This template was created through the participation of 32 different races in the distant future, but failed most catastrophically as communication between the diverse parts broke down. The warfare that resulted destroyed several planets, leaving their souls without a place to re-incarnate.

A solution was required that would not only provide a home for these displaced souls, but the environment in which the template could be applied and the incompatibilities resolved. In devising a way for this design to succeed, it was decided to create a loop in time and to have those souls who no longer had planets incarnate back into the distant past, completing lifetime after lifetime in the loop to learn the lessons needed for the future to succeed when next we catch up to it. The earth was chosen to provide the solution.

It did not seem likely that the lessons could be better learned at a level denser than the higher one we had in the future (we have descended in frequency from the loss of energy caused by the shock), but we had an ace up our sleeve. From the incredible trauma, our emotional bodies shattered and formed the sub-personalities of man. Each of us has within our individual psyches the components we had as a multi-racial empire in the future. We can thus learn the lessons needed for the diversity to flourish within unity in the future, by reincarnating and studying these inner pieces.

Man not only has these races represented in his emotional aspects, but in the genetic components of his DNA. All races are represented that were part of this future template that would eventually become the template for not only this part of the galaxy, but the whole universe. Even the hostile enemy has contributed to our DNA. The 32 races that were part of this future, however, are themselves representative of the 32 root races of the universe. It is as though man has gathered together all the strings of the weaving of Creation within his DNA. But Creation is a reflection of the Infinite, and in this way man has become the microcosm of the macrocosm.

As we shall see later, when we reach the stage of Immortal Master in our progression, we gain the ability to upload our insights directly to the Infinite and the future no longer need be so turbulent. In this way we directly shape the way the future unfolds.

This solution can bring the equilibrium necessary to move into oneness, but where will the momentum come from? The body of man is the sacred crucible where alchemy can change us to something akin to anti-matter; something that doesn't seem to belong in

Creation (which is <u>negatively</u> charged as a whole), a <u>positively</u> charged being. When this happens, all of Creation is pulled to where we are (at the edge of the donut in the densest levels) because opposite poles <u>attract</u> in energy and matter. The pressure once again builds, as more and more of us fulfill our destiny as the alchemists of the cosmos, until life is pushed over the edge on the blue road home.

The loop of time we have been traveling on is said by the Toltecs to span 18 million years. The star beings that occasionally visit my classes have said the races came together to create the composite beings of humanity 10 million years ago. We are clearly in the home stretch where this painful loop of lifetimes will end. So much responsibility has rested and does rest on our shoulders–but we are the leaders of tomorrow and the leaders of the past. The task is so important that we have come from the highest levels of this universe to participate in it. We have created lives where every moment is fraught with meaning and on every decision the future pivots. Let us carry this great responsibility with the utmost awareness, moment by moment. Great is the epic in which we have vital parts and greater still the glory, for we are the architects of a new tomorrow.

The Sequences Of Creation

There is a pulse within the cosmos; a Creation cycle of expansion and contraction, during which the unknown portions of the Infinite's being are explored. It can be equated to the circulation system of the human body. The blood flowing away from the heart is likened to the expansion cycle, called the red road; and the contraction, or return of the blood to the heart, the blue road home. We have been on a cosmic red road, an exploratory journey of expansion, with this lower dimension of physicality now being near the edge of the tube torus.

Within a human's body, information is gathered by the chakras which gather seven different levels of light or information, which is then downloaded to the endocrine system and transported by the blood (the venous system) to the heart where it is translated as 'feelings' by the thymus. The brain observes these many different feelings, decides which ones need to be explored and then interprets them.

Because of the density and distortion required to provide enough resistance to propel us over the edge of this tube torus of Creation and back to the heart of God, a unique creation was conceived. This creation–lower man–would mirror the whole within its form and fields and communicate directly to the Infinite. When this complex being enters the stage of an Immortal Master in the flesh it becomes the I AM that I AM, able to help design the unfolding of the cosmos by contributing its collective experiences directly to the Infinite. The rest of Creation's experiential knowledge is downloaded once it begins to return on the blue road home, but we have the opportunity to help shape the return journey now. (See Figure 1, The Sequences of Creation)

The Infinite

As the information of an Immortal Master uploads to the I AM, the I AM gains perception and luminosity (light is accessed information). Any being can only contain so much light before it must transfigure into the next phase of its evolution. When transfiguring occurs, there is a tremendous release of energy (the markings on the Shroud of Turin were burnt into the cloth when Christ's body was transfigured into a resurrected being).

The Sequences of Creation

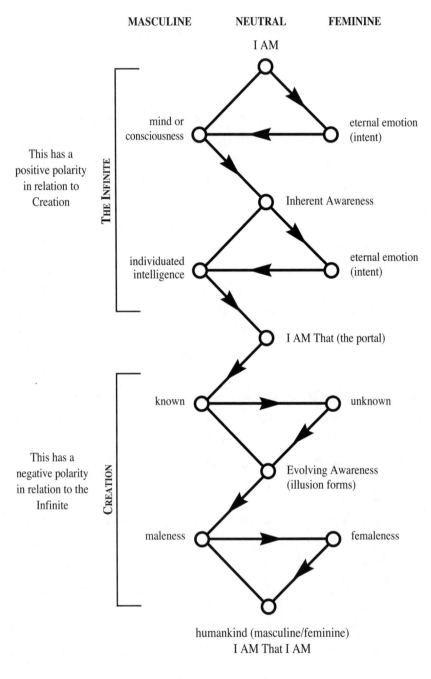

(Figure 1)

The energy released from the I AM awakens emotion. A desire to know itself stirs and exerts pressure upon mind. The movement of desire is that which we know as <u>time</u>, the <u>first building block of Creation.</u>

In order for us to speak about the next building block that forms, we need to explain the use of certain terms:

• **Consciousness**–this can be described as mind at rest or both the known and the unknown intermingled and undifferentiated. Think of this as a mountain containing coal, diamonds and dirt all mixed together, solid and ancient.

• **Intelligence**–exhibits the ability to choose between two things. Everything boils down to only one choice: what is life-enhancing and what is not. Think of intelligence as that which allows the miner to choose the diamonds over the coal.

• **Awareness**–the word awareness indicates that one is wary or attentive. Being aware means to be watchful and wide awake. Our level of awareness determines how much we are likely to learn from our experiences. Think of awareness as the way the miner studies in detail the buckets of dirt he hauls out of the mountain to find the diamonds he searches for.

When consciousness, or mind at rest, is awakened by the prodding of Creation's emotion desiring to know itself, it awakens only in the area 'touched' by the emotion. In other words, if there is an ocean of mind and the storms occur only in the area of high winds, a space has been created that has a different quality (stormy) than the rest of the ocean. Thus where emotion ripples across the surface of mind, space is created. <u>Space</u> is the <u>second building block of Creation.</u>

Mind now remembers all previous Creational cycles and their insights, adding any new ones gained at this level of density. It exercises intelligence to understand and, compelled by the desire to know itself, gains so much insight and information that it can no longer contain such luminosity.

It implodes and in the next instant explodes into the Big Bang, releasing vast amounts of energy, which fuse the mental and emotional components into a type of awareness called Inherent Awareness. Inherent Awareness moves outward from its point of origin in straight lines forever and ever. The energy released spreads across space. Thus the third building block forms–energy.

Life has now pushed into a lower band of frequency and at this level again, the strong emotion that wants to explore the unknown portions of its being creates a powerful frequency of desire. The frequency, like the song of a harpist, vibrates across awareness and clusters it. A kind of very refined 'matter' forms (at this point materialization as we know it has not yet formed) as it individuates and is able to relate to its parts. The fourth building block is matter.

Creation

And now through the light of the I AM shining through time, space, energy and matter, the reflection of light and dark forms a mirror in which the Infinite can examine itself. Though the explanation of exactly how the Infinite forms Creation will be given later, at this point we only need to know that Creation is formed by the power behind the Infinite's emotion or intent to know itself. The Infinite splits its field in two, like a cell dividing, and forms the field in which Creation will take place.

The first act within Creation was an act of intelligence: to separate that which was known from that which was unknown. Thus polarity was formed, the known being the positive pole and the unknown being the negative pole. One third of the individuated beings that entered into Creation at this point underwent a voluntary forgetfulness of the joy and the oneness and the light that is their true nature as they volunteered to play the unyielded light on the stage of Creation.

One third of the lights of heaven were dimmed in that moment because of their inclusiveness and their belief in the importance of the evolution of awareness. As they fell in consciousness, all Creation fell with them and a new awareness was born: Evolving Awareness. The straight outward movement of Inherent Awareness moved outward still, but now in spiral form. Time slowed down, allowing us again and again to have the opportunity to learn the insights we have contracted to explore.

The next phase of Creation is the forming of material life to incorporate the unknown into the known through experience. Like a caterpillar on the edge of a leaf, we take bites out of the unknown through our experience. And as the caterpillar that transmutes the leaf into energy for itself and then transfigures within its chrysalis, discarding that which it no longer needs, we use our transmuting of the unknown into the known as an energy source. We then have the energy to transfigure into a life form beyond our current one. In material life we can transfigure into spiritualized and immortal matter by evolving our awareness.

In order to explore the unknown, material life divides maleness from femaleness so that the unknown, which is part of the femaleness of Creation, can be further separated out for exploration. In manifestation, males and females mirror this further separation of opposite poles, that they may study their own male and female inner pieces within each other.

In order to illustrate these sequences of Creation, 3-D geometry is used. The cosmos functions through dynamic geometry, however, that has no angles and no joints.[1] The drawings give the impres-

1 Detailed explanations are given in *Journey to the Heart of God III* and *Path to Freedom III* CD sets.

sion of separate pieces, but we never have been separate from that great and mighty Source that sustains us. Cosmic rays from which atoms form, flow like unfathomable rivers through all time and space and penetrate the densest matter. We are and always have been part of an all encompassing God of light. From knowing this with every fiber of our being, our hearts can find the safety to burst forth with a love to help heal the wounds of alienation in all humanity.

"Truth is needed first, and where it is present there love will be also... If you hold your mind on the good news of how you and I relate, how we are inseparably one... Understanding will fill your mind with a vision so beautiful, so desirable, so attainable, that you will never have to try to love me. Love will flood your mind and heart spontaneously every time you think of this great vision."[2]

Dynamic Geometry

The geometric models we use to explain cosmic evolution and relationships use the static, illusion-based geometry of this density. We depend on platonic solids and geometry with angles and joints to get our point across. Within the true geometry of the cosmos such things do not exist.

There are no static objects in life. Everything is part of the great flow of the river of outpouring life, and light flows in a way that has no angles and no joints. The angles and joints are part of the illusion. Light flows in a way that incorporates all our platonic shapes, but it is simply a trick of the eye.

For example, set up two pencils attached in the following way to the edge of a table: the first pencil stands straight up from the edge of the table at a 90 degree angle. The next pencil is attached

2 From *The Door of Everything* by Ruby Nelson.

to the top of the first pencil also at a 90 degree angle to the other pencil, but facing more towards you (i.e., sticking out over the edge of the table). If you now stand above your construction, it appears that the top pencil is in fact touching the table in a perfect triangle.[3] (See Figure 2, The Way Dynamic Geometry Works)

Another example is the bottom of the creational triangles. It represents the cosmos and is not flat, but rather the bottom of a figure eight in the interrelationship of its various components. If we depict just the bottom of the figure eight, we would draw the zero point circle and two downward pointing triangles to illustrate the two trinities within created life. If we use a dark enough marker, and fold our paper over so that the circle of the zero point lines up with the lowest circle, we can see a star tetrahedron if we hold our paper against the light. It appears to have touching edges and joints, even though the triangles are not even on the same plane.

Light bounces off barriers or fields (such as the edge of the space designated for this outbreath of God) in a way that gives them the appearance of a solid shape even though they are not.

Although further and deeper information is given as footnoted, we mention it here so that the reader is aware that the illustrations given represent relationships only and should not be taken at face value.

In dynamic geometry one shape changes into another in one continuous flow.

Man's Destiny—The Sub-Personalities

The template the creator gods of this universe designed to bring the diverse races into harmony is based on unity within diversity.

---

3 Readers are referred to the recordings of *Journey to the Heart of God, III* for much deeper, more detailed descriptions of dynamic geometry within Creation.

The Way Dynamic Geometry Works

Example A

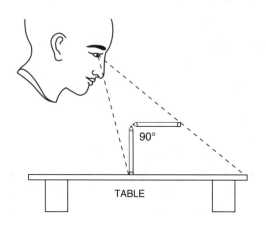

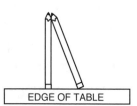

EDGE OF TABLE

To the eye it appears like a triangle even though objects aren't on the same plane.

Example B

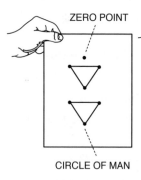

ZERO POINT

CIRCLE OF MAN

Step 1:
Draw the triangles of the trinities of life within Creation.

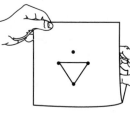

Step 2:
Fold the paper over. The circle of man goes behind the zero point.

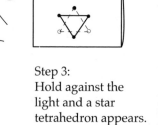

Step 3:
Hold against the light and a star tetrahedron appears.

Geometric shapes appearing as having angles and joints are but a trick of the eye.

(Figure 2)

It was first tested in the future before the loop of time was created. Our earth was chosen because of its location at the edge of the space allotted for Creation's expansion. At the edge, the greatest density and the largest diversity exist. If unity could be achieved here, it would most certainly be able to succeed anywhere else.

The explosive destruction of the future dynasty came in part as a result of the various races not being able to see each other's contribution and value. The tremendous differences in the way reality was being accessed made communication almost impossible. The failure to make the leap from the social stage of diversity to the next level of unity within diversity created stagnation of growth. Rage is used to break up stagnation within the cosmos, and the dynasty attracted the rage of conquering races.

From the trauma, the emotional bodies of the victims who had lost their planets were fractured. As previously mentioned, these became the spirits that incarnated back in time as man, learning the lessons through their incarnations that would benefit and change the future. Their emotional fragments became the sub-personalities of man. Thus, through the perfection of this plan, humankind mirrors the diverse factions present in the future.

Learning the unique value of each of our sub-personalities and allowing each one to express in its own individual way, we receive the opportunity to explore unity within diversity. A small trickle of information regarding the inner warrior, inner sage, inner child and inner nurturer is finding its way into mainstream thinking. The interaction between these pieces of the psyche, however, is seldom understood and as a result most people are not integrated.

The qualities generally exhibited by humankind of moodiness, depression, irrationality, lack of stability and dependability, as well as a deep reservoir of pain, are in large part the result of their alienation from these inner sub-personalities. Even those who work hard to achieve personal power can find that to neglect putting these pieces into their proper function can produce the pitfall of ego because the inner pieces demand recognition.

The forming of the sub-personalities of man has helped him become that unique creature previously mentioned: the microcosm of the macrocosm. Within the Infinite and its Creation, the four trinities represent the sub-personalities of the One expressing as the Many. The Primary Trinity is the inner warrior; the Creative Trinity is the inner sage. Within Creation, the Trinity of Indwelling Life is the inner child and the Trinity of Materialization is the inner nurturer. In the future, various races represented the different sub-personalities. (See Figure 3, Relationship of Sub-Personalities)

The sub-personalities receive truth about the known and unknown portions of the cosmos in a specific way. In addition, each needs to express in its own allotted time; the child being allowed to play, the nurturer to nurture, etc. Each receives from another sub-personality its input and guidance and each communicates its insights to yet another sub-personality. As these personalities access, interpret and organize the information from their environment, the unknown is turned into the known in a very specific way. Like an assembly line, the unknown gets handed from one personality to the next until it is turned into the known.

The first one to contribute to the solving of an unknown stimulus is the nurturer. It uses altered perception (such as meditation, dreaming during sleep, etc.) to obtain symbols regarding a situation it may want to know about; for instance, the trustworthiness of a new business associate. As the nurturer goes into an altered state (with practice one can move in and out of it rapidly–even in a business meeting) the image of a blackbird might flash across the screen of the mind. This symbol is passed on to the inner child. The inner child feels the blackbird pertains to the new business

Relationship of Sub-personalities

Within Social Structures or Human Psyche

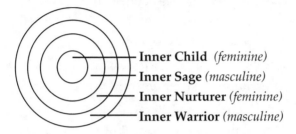

Inner Child *(feminine)*
Inner Sage *(masculine)*
Inner Nurturer *(feminine)*
Inner Warrior *(masculine)*

Each circle is responsible to oversee the welfare of the circle(s) within it.

The Route of Communication between the Sub-personalities

Inner Warrior
- Receives interpretation of non-cognitive feelings from Inner Sage
- Communicates to Inner Nurturer when it is safe for vulnerable parts to express and creates strategy for the inner family

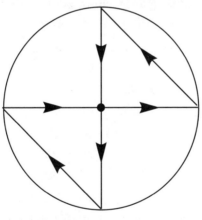

Inner Child
- Expresses its unanalyzed feelings to Inner Sage
- Receives parenting from Inner Nurturer and its dreaming impressions

Inner Sage
- Receives Inner Child's feelings and interprets them
- Communicates deductions to Inner Warrior to act upon

Inner Nurturer
- Receives information from Inner Warrior as to when Inner Child can express and strategy for inner family
- Communicates with Inner Child in a loving parental role

(Figure 3)

associate's lawyer and feels an insecurity coming from the associate. It feels uncomfortable and would like to be outside playing.

The inner sage receives from the child not only the nurturer's contribution, but its feelings about the situation. Its job as sage is to analyze all this non-cognitive information and, seeing behind the appearances, interpret what is really going on. The child felt the bird only around the lawyer. In right brain's language, a blackbird stands for treacherous thoughts. Even though the child liked the associate, the insecurity of the associate means the lawyer will be the one making the decisions. The end result is that the child felt the situation should be avoided. In examining the details, the sage realizes that even when the questions presented to the associate were not legal ones, he would still ask the lawyer's opinion before answering. This outside circumstance further confirms that the lawyer will determine the relationship.

The analysis of the details and the conclusion about the associate are passed on to the next personality in the assembly line, the inner warrior. Its job is to take the details passed on by the sage and put them into the larger picture; a lot like putting most of a puzzle together and being able to deduce the finished picture even though there are still puzzle pieces missing.

The warrior realizes that he will need to hire the best lawyers to watch the opposing lawyer during the initial negotiations to prevent treachery. The warrior weighs the benefits of what the associate brings to the table against the burdens. The treacherous lawyer will no longer be able to have influence once they join forces, as the existing legal team will be taking over. The associate's indecisiveness can be compensated for with a strong support team and has the advantage that at least he will not constantly be pulling in an opposite direction. The warrior decides to proceed with the business relationship.

The warrior is the strategist. The sage is the analyst. The child and nurturer are the undercover investigating team, gathering information behind the scenes.

In the future dynasty, the child races knew an enemy was infiltrating key areas of the civilizations and that an invasion was imminent but their attempts to communicate this to the warriors failed due to the breakdown in the 'assembly line'. One can imagine the following scenario as an illustration:

The child races might have gone to the warriors and said, "We have a bad feeling about the future." The warriors, being very left-brained, would want facts. "What is it about the future that gives you this feeling?" The reply would be, "We don't know, but it's something awful." Since it's not the child races' job to analyze, the warriors would therefore devalue their input and tell them to come back when they had some answers. The child races would feel unheard and eventually not share their feelings at all.

If on the other hand, the child races went to the sages, one child race might say, "We have a bad feeling about the future". Another might have a bad feeling about the sky and yet another might have a dread because the nurturer race told them it dreamed about the planet disappearing after an explosion. The sage race would conclude that a future invasion from space would annihilate a planet, relay that conclusion to the warriors who would then design a defense strategy.

Much is at stake in our quest to understand our inner pieces. The future depends on it and the universe depends on the success of the future template. If we cannot learn the harmonious interaction of our sub-personalities, we will not have the necessary insights to change the future when we meet it again. That would mean we would have to again repeat this intensely painful loop. It doesn't have to be this hard–the future is determined by our choices today.

The Flow Of Communication

The more we master the inner dynamics of the sub-personalities, the more we contribute to the success of the future and its peaceful resolution for the unity of diverse cultures. In other words, we can solve the problems of the macrocosm within, because a human being is in every aspect representative of the whole.

The balancing and expression of the sub-personalities was the task of the adept in many ancient mystery schools, such as the ones in Egypt. The task of the initiate was to cut the ties of social conditioning and the hold past experience had on him. Only then did he progress to work with the sub-personalities as an adept. This was in preparation for the next level, mastery of the mind. In this way the bodies of man were cleared from physical and etheric (initiate), to emotional (adept), to mental (mastery). This prepared the student for the breakdown of the barrier between the four lower bodies of man and the three higher bodies. (See Figure 4, The Seven Bodies of Man) This allows the free-flowing exchange of energy between all seven bodies that occurs once we have made the transition from God-consciousness to Ascended Mastery.

If the adept stage is skipped, the student will invariably trip up and succumb to power's traps during the stage of mastery. The need to impress or to prove ourselves occurs through a dysfunctional inner child. The need to judge occurs when the sage is dysfunctional. The need to attack others with our increased abilities speaks of a dysfunctional warrior, and the saving of others happens when the nurturer has abandoned the needs of its own inner family in favor of outside recognition. This is the single greatest reason so many spiritual teachers become egocentric or judgmental at the very time when they should have been able to transition into God-consciousness.

The Seven Bodies of Man

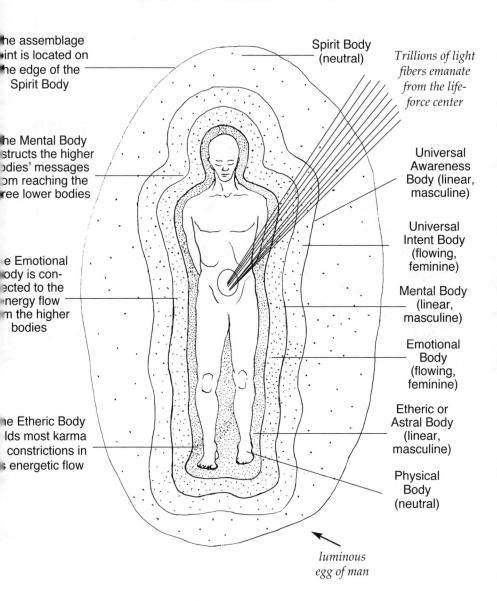

The assemblage point is located on the edge of the Spirit Body

The Mental Body obstructs the higher bodies' messages from reaching the three lower bodies

The Emotional Body is connected to the energy flow from the higher bodies

The Etheric Body holds most karma & constrictions in its energetic flow

Spirit Body (neutral)

Trillions of light fibers emanate from the life-force center

Universal Awareness Body (linear, masculine)

Universal Intent Body (flowing, feminine)

Mental Body (linear, masculine)

Emotional Body (flowing, feminine)

Etheric or Astral Body (linear, masculine)

Physical Body (neutral)

luminous egg of man

The bodies are superimposed over each other and form the luminous egg (cocoon) of man. The trillions of light fibers from the lifeforce center penetrate all other bodies forming the luminous egg.

(Figure 4)

55

Let us therefore practice the interaction of the sub-personalities with the diligence their importance deserves. The primary flow of information (this does not mean that personalities cannot also randomly communicate with each other) is as follows:

1. The nurturer relays the strategy designed by the warrior to the inner family. It also tells the child about signs in the inner or outer environment about which to gather feelings;

2. The child gathers non-cognitive information about indwelling life or the unknown. It adds its feelings surrounding the nurturer's discernment. It does not indulge in trying to figure it out, but passes it on to the sage for analysis;

3. The sage then communicates to the warrior whether there is a threat or any other degree of unease about a situation. It looks behind the appearances for its assessment;

4. The warrior puts it in context with previous communications from the sage and provides the more vulnerable pieces with guidelines of expression–how and when it is appropriate to express.

The True Nature Of The Seven Directions

It is from the mental body that a succession of bodies form, eventually culminating in the physical body. It is so not only for man, that unique micro-cosmos, but for the Infinite. Just as in man, the mental, emotional, etheric (astral) and physical bodies of the Infinite have certain qualities that set them apart from one another, and these qualities give rise to the four directions. (See Figure 5, The Seven Directions)

The mental body of the Infinite includes within it the Primary Trinity, but it gives rise to Inherent Awareness, (the trinity thus becomes a square). The mental body is therefore represented by a

The Seven Directions

The Four Directions

The Infinite's Four Lower Bodies

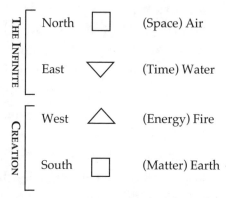

Used exclusively by a being in identity consciousness

The Three Additional Directions

The Infinite's Three Higher Bodies

Within
(Original
Awareness)

Below (Love)

Above (Light)

Original Awareness, Love and Light are the building blocks from which all existence forms along with Time, Space, Energy and Matter. A being in expanded awareness functions from all seven directions.

☐ = masculine   △ = feminine

(Figure 5)

square and is masculine. It represents space and the direction of North. It holds the large vision for the other bodies.

The emotional body is feminine in relation to the mental body and is creative in nature. It is the Creative Trinity which gives birth to Creation and is represented by a triangle. It represents the flow of the Infinite's emotion (the desire to know itself) and the movement of this flow is time. By creating a deliberate counter-clockwise spin to the emotion, it fractures the Infinite into two: the Infinite and its Creation. The direction it represents, the East, uses analysis to pierce illusion.

Both directions located within the Infinite are masculine in relation to that which it creates. Where then lies the true 'Mother in Heaven'? And does Creation always have to be 'unreal', only a mirror image of the mental and emotional bodies of the Infinite? There is a most glorious answer to these questions, never before revealed to humankind, and a happy ending to man's sacrifice and suffering upon the altar of furthering evolution.

Let us first look at the other two bodies of the Infinite, those that fall within Creation: the etheric (astral) and physical bodies. These bodies represent (indwelling life) and (life manifested) or materialization.[4]

The etheric body of the Infinite is what we refer to as the higher self, or the Trinity of Indwelling Life. It is that which interprets the Infinite's purpose into form and experience. It is feminine in relation to all other bodies.

Although it designs and gives birth to material life, it is not the mother that we seek in order to alleviate the suffering and make us 'real'. The etheric body of the Infinite falls into the realm of the mirror image. It too is but a reflection or 'unreal'. Besides, its primary task is to manifest the Infinite's purpose, not to listen to the

4 See topic on *The Power of Emotion.*

way we (material life) would wish to have it.

The etheric body holds all unresolved pieces of previous experience. It represents the West, the direction of energy. Being feminine, it is represented by a triangle. It works with frequency to manifest the purpose of the Infinite. It splits itself in order to create manifestation (material life) and forms the Trinity of Materialization. (See Figure 6, The Seven Directions Within the Mother of All, the Infinite and Creation)

The Trinity of materialization is the physical body of the Infinite–the cosmos. Its purpose is to explore the unknown through experience and it represents the South. It is masculine in relation to higher self or the Trinity of Indwelling Life. It lives out the purpose of the Infinite to explore existence by manifesting as much diversity of form as possible.

Within this trinity a new awareness forms: Evolving Awareness. Instead of the linear movement of Inherent Awareness formed within the Infinite, this awareness spirals and with the birth of this additional child, the 3 becomes a 4 and so the Trinity of Materialization is represented as a square.

The four bodies of the Infinite and its Creation are the same bodies used primarily by a human being in identity consciousness. Someone in identity consciousness tries to run his or her life using these bodies alone. In other words, there is a two dimensional quality to life lived with only four bodies fully participating. The four directions expressed and in balance still keep us in identity consciousness.

Information not previously known during this cycle of life on earth is that the Infinite and its Creation (the four lower bodies of the Infinite) sprang from three higher bodies, the spiritual-emotional, spiritual-mental and spirit bodies. (See Figure 7, The Seven Elements of the Seven Directions)

The Seven Directions Within the Mother of All, the Infinite and Creation

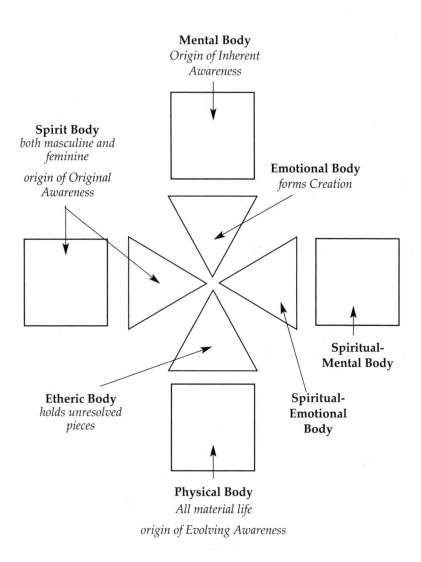

Mental Body
Origin of Inherent Awareness

Spirit Body
both masculine and feminine

origin of Original Awareness

Emotional Body
forms Creation

Spiritual-Mental Body

Etheric Body
holds unresolved pieces

Spiritual-Emotional Body

Physical Body
All material life

origin of Evolving Awareness

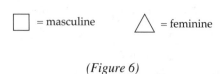

☐ = masculine △ = feminine

(Figure 6)

60

The Seven Elements of the Seven Directions
Within the Seven Bodies of the Infinite

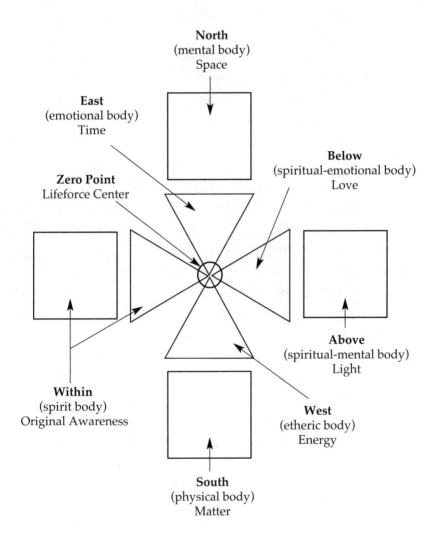

(Figure 7)

The spiritual-emotional body is feminine and is represented by a triangle. It represents the direction of below and the element of love–one of the three original elements from which the Infinite and its Creation sprang (not the same as the emotion of love).

The spiritual-mental body is masculine and represented by a square. It represents the direction of above and the element of light, the second building block of all that is.

The spirit body is neutral in that it is both masculine and feminine, represented by a square and a triangle. It is the direction of within and consists of the third building block from which the Infinite sprang: Original Awareness. The spirit body of the Infinite, like the spirit body of any organism, contains the possibilities waiting to become. The Infinite's spirit body, just like that of man,[5] contains trillions and trillions of lightfibers of possibilities outside of itself waiting to become. The spirit body holds the key to the next evolutionary stage of the vast Being we are apart of.

Jointly the three higher bodies of the Infinite form a feminine trinity that birthed what we know as God (the Infinite) and is the true Mother of God. When the four lower bodies open to the influence from this true Goddess, her love spiritualizes matter and it becomes 'real', immortalized matter.

Immortal Mastery requires the bringing forth of light into every action. It requires the complete silencing of thought, our actions guided by Original Awareness–that effortless knowing the world calls genius. This form of awareness, Original Awareness, is the third awareness.

The Third Awareness

For eons the Toltec seers have spoken about the two types of awareness within the Infinite and its Creation–Inherent Awareness

5 For greater detail of the seven bodies of man, see *A Life of Miracles*, page 104.

and Evolving Awareness. It was not until the unlocking of the mystery showing three other frequency bands or 'bodies' existed beyond the four previously known, that yet another mystery revealed itself. A third form of awareness emerged. Previously it was known that the masculine awareness, Inherent Awareness, had given birth to the feminine awareness, Evolving Awareness. It was now found that the newly discovered third form of awareness had sired Inherent Awareness. (See Figure 8, Three Types of Awareness)

Inherent Awareness moves in a straight line, outward from its source. Evolving Awareness curves that straight line into spirals moving outward forever away from the source. If we live a life that is learning from experience, the spirals of awareness in our life get larger and larger 'hoops'. If we on the other hand, live fruitless lives not learning from experience, we have smaller and smaller rings or spirals in terms of diameter.

The third type of awareness which we shall call Original Awareness is neutral in that it is both masculine and feminine. Original Awareness springs from the three higher bodies of the Infinite and is both masculine and feminine and thus neutral. Inherent and Evolving Awareness spring from the four lower bodies.

The one thing all three types of awareness have in common is movement. Original Awareness moves in an arc, a large curve combining the forward thrust of Inherent Awareness with the curving found in Evolving Awareness. Since Original Awareness is neutral it has both masculine characteristics, the forward linear movement, and feminine qualities in that it curves or makes a large arc.

The huge significance of this third awareness is that without it we could not expand and contract in creational cycles. Without it we would never be able to return to Source; the outbreath of God would never become the inbreath. It is the source of all awareness

Three Types of Awareness

Original Awareness
Movement: It arcs
Originates: Within the Spirit Body
Polarity: Neutral
Location: It moves through all 7 bodies

Inherent Awareness
Movement: A straight line
Originates: Within the Mental Body
Polarity: Masculine
Location: It moves through the 4 lower bodies

Evolving Awareness
Movement: It spirals
Originates: Within the Physical Body
Polarity: Feminine
Location: It moves through the physical body

The three types of awareness create the tube torus of the Infinite and its Creation. It exists of trillions of arcing spirals propelling away from and returning to Source or originating point.

(Figure 8)

as we know it and the only connection life within the Infinite has with anything it has not yet experienced that lies within the realm of possibilities.

In the same way that the luminous cocoon of man holds the light fibers of all possible life that could conceivably be experienced, so too do all possibilities that are available to the Infinite and Creation lie as fibers of light within the Spirit Body of the Infinite. It is in the Spirit Body of the Infinite (also in the Spirit Body of man) where Original Awareness is born. It is from here the divine perfection of life unfolding is governed in order and harmony; it is from here the inexpressible power that maintains and upholds not only Creation, but the Infinite itself, stems.

The Anatomy Of Change

As awareness moves outward through the cosmos in spiraling arcs, our lives move with it. The cycles in our lives are linked to the cycles of the spirals. There are small cycles within larger ones. The only constant we encounter in life is that everything changes: awareness always moves.

As we go through either the smaller changes in our lives or the larger, more dramatic ones, a pattern starts to emerge; a map we can use to identify what stage of change we're in. Each cycle goes through three distinct phases, identifiable by their symptoms.

Transformation:

As we grow in awareness and problems are recognized for what they truly are (opportunities for growth), they lose their hold on us and we no longer need them. Suddenly circumstances in our lives seem to change. Friendships fall by the wayside, jobs may become obsolete and we find life flowing a lot more effortlessly as it transforms before our eyes.

This stage is marked by so many changes that it can be called the time of the death of the old. If we hold on longer than we should to relationships or situations, we find life shedding them for us through forced change. This time can certainly be disconcerting as the old platform we stood on disintegrates, but the energy released when that which no longer serves us drops away, is a great reward. With increased energy comes new experiences and ease in meeting old challenges that bring a sense of deep self-satisfaction. As one sheds the old, the body responds by purifying itself. Toxins release and the body can hold more light.

Transmutation:

After transformation sheds the unnecessary parts of our lives, the true challenges stand revealed. This phase is the one where most people get stuck. Mindlessly feeling victimized by the very experiences their higher selves designed for them, they fail to turn pain to wisdom, judgment to compassion. The very essence of transmutation is to turn something of a lower frequency into a higher frequency; the alchemical process of turning lead to gold.

During the phase of transmutation, we are confronted with never before encountered challenges or those we have failed to learn from. Life has just served the ball across the net and waits for our response. The harder the serve, the more we can gain. Most people spend their whole life running away from the balls coming across the net instead of hitting them back.

If we can find the lessons and insights of our challenges, we score enough points to move on to the next game. If we are very diligent, we can even gain insights on behalf of others, increasing our points on the scoreboard. The insights we gain during this stage must be tested to turn them into experiential knowledge.

Transfiguration:

Major transfigurations such as disconnecting from ego-identification (becoming God-conscious) and entering into Immortal Mastery come but a few times in one's life. All change, however, follows this exact map with its three stages. The larger transfigurations are just more noticeable. Even the little changes add up, eventually allowing enough light into our lives for our entire life to transfigure. As more and more clarity is gained, the person must transfigure in order to accommodate the increased light.

The joyous truth is that there is no end to progression. When we have made it through all the evolutionary stages of man's awareness, we shall move even beyond that ultimate goal of humanness: Immortal Mastery. Beyond lies the god kingdom where we can come and go with the speed of thought throughout all realms of time and space–the cosmos as our playground.

CHAPTER TWO

SECRETS OF TRANSFIGURATION

Stages In The Evolution Of Awareness

In ancient Egypt there were specific temples to guide truth seekers dedicated to the spiritual path, through the stages of the evolution of awareness. They were built in a logarithmic spiral, culminating in the place where man might transcend the stages altogether and move into the next level of being, the god-kingdom. This event that lay even beyond ascension, took place in the great pyramid of Giza.

The stages of man have never varied. They are part of our human condition and truth seekers today face the same testings and initiations man has always faced.

Stage 1: Ego-Identification

Phase 1. The Initiate (Transformation). In the initiate's phase, there is an emptying out of old beliefs and ideas. The student becomes aware of the old programming that has shaped his reality. He starts to loosen the grip of social conditioning and becomes aware of his identities he has so relied on. In this phase, the initiate begins to acquaint himself with tools used for discernment and learns which to use for the known and for the unknown.

The result of these increased insights and new skills is that the mind achieves more order. The more the mind is trained and the more the prison bars of old belief systems dissolve, the more energy becomes available. Everything the initiate has taken for granted is now questioned. The greater the realization that he knows nothing for certain, the greater are his chances of success upon the path to ascension. Spiritual growth accelerates during this phase and old relationships will either start to reject him or he will start to shed them as no longer relevant to his life.

The testing of this phase comes when fear arises as the old, safe parameters of his world disappear. It is disconcerting to find life's foundations, like a belief in good and evil, dissolve before one's eyes. Finding most of what he held onto so tightly to be illusion will either send the initiate scampering fearfully back to his prison cell, or help him take a leap of faith over the edge of the cliff into the unknown.

Phase 2. The Adept (Transmutation). The adept is beginning to become quite proficient at wielding the tools of awareness. He is aware of how limited his knowledge is and as a result other realities begin to open.

He starts to see symbolically, no longer taking his world at face value, and becomes literate at reading the signs in his environment. The world becomes his teacher as it speaks to him.

One of the key insights of this phase is the loss of feeling victimized. The adept sees instead how he has co-created each event to help him fulfill his destiny. Challenges become welcome sources of insight, which in turn yield power. There is a greater feeling of stability in this phase as the rewards are more immediate and discernable.

The power surges that accompany the insights his new-found tools help him extract from challenges can be exhilarating. No longer does he shun these sources of power the way the rest of the world does, but instead welcomes them. The larger the challenges, the greater the rewards, until he can feel himself grow more and more powerful.

The surges of power he now regularly experiences release physical excretions within the endocrine system, triggering feelings much like the thrill the gambler gets. His testing now comes as he finds himself becoming addicted to the thrill of challenge.

To help prevent this pitfall from snaring him and stopping his progression, he must now change his focus to balancing the sub-personalities within. The balancing of the sub-personalities is not only the task of the adept, it is also his salvation. As he works diligently on parenting his inner child and learning about his inner nurturer, for instance, it takes his mind off the pursuit of challenge and helps him take himself less seriously.

Phase 3. The Master (Transfiguration). The master has a formidable task to accomplish. As this is the last phase remaining in identity consciousness (ego-identification), he must gather enough power and energy to make the big leap of entirely disconnecting from ego and enter into God-consciousness.

The training of this phase emphasizes the streamlining of the master's life. The conservation of energy is essential and must become a part of life. All initial energy is used up by a disorganized left brain. Only the surplus is available to the right brain to access the unknown. At this point the master's mind must become so organized that energy is freely available to access more and more of the unseen realms.

The unseen world, once accessed, can be very seductive. It is valuable as a tool to loosen the iron grip of the rational mind, but it can also become a pitfall in two ways:

• The lure of this vast unseen reality can easily divert the master's attention from where his real supply of power lies–his everyday challenges and relationships. Instead of building his power supply for the task ahead, he could become more and more aloof and arrogant as his reality takes on vast dimensions beyond those of his fellow man. He could withdraw from everyday life, stifling his spiritual growth even as his abilities increase.

• When someone becomes aware of the unseen worlds, the unseen worlds also become aware of him. Entities of all types (some call themselves guides) are attracted to the master and offer their skills to assist him. The more the master focuses on them, the more his energy is given to them. The ease with which they can materialize objects, see the future or other people's lives, prevents the master from developing those skills himself. Particularly if the sub-personalities were not 'hooked up' in the previous stage, the inner child's need for recognition will come to lure the master into using his allies to gain recognition and applause from others. At the very moment when the master should be free from identity, a new one (such as master, shaman, saint, etc.) arises and he is unable to proceed to God-consciousness.

It is during this phase that the purpose with which the student embarked on this path makes a very large difference. If his purpose was power, this is the end of his spiritual progress. If his purpose was to seek perception, he has a good chance of slipping past the lure of power as long as he keeps his eyes firmly and unwaveringly on his goal. Tempted by power, learning to conserve energy, the master prepares for the large leap of entirely disconnecting from identifying with the limited self–the stage of God-consciousness in which he is called a seer.

As the time approaches for this momentous event that occurs in a moment, the master feels more and more disconnected. He views his life and actions as though from a distance and his perception becomes more objective. Value judgments of what is desirable and what is not, fall away.

Stage 2: God-Consciousness

Phase 1. The Emptiness (Transformation). As in the first phase of ego-identification, this is the phase of emptying out. But unlike the initiate's phase, it happens suddenly and without conscious effort. The seer in this first phase knows he is no-thing; emptied of thoughts and most common emotions except for an overwhelming loneliness that recognizes that there is no being besides himself in existence.

At times he is as vast as the cosmos and at other times he crashes back into the body and feels claustrophobic at the confinement. The fear that he may not find his body at all is strong during the first few weeks. Although he has lost identity, he must retain self-awareness or he will plunge into insanity. As it is, in the absence of the inner dialogue he feels as though he has lost his mind (and he has–his surface mind).

For one who has had concussion, the feeling is very similar. Information does not imprint. In other words, one cannot retain what one decided half an hour ago and so one either has to write everything down or keep making the same decision over and over again.

Linear time is meaningless. Physical activity slows down enormously. If life would allow it, the seer in this phase would just sit. It's too much effort to talk and interact. Physical energy is very low as he learns to traverse inner space instead.

Because the stages differ from each other only in that they are one spiral up in awareness, their three phases exhibit similar qualities. As in the first phase of ego-identification, the first phase within God-consciousness has as its testing, fear. Some enter into this phase but because they fear their duties won't be done (which is not the case–even though their old way of thinking no longer exists, duties are done without thought when they should be), they retreat. Fear at relinquishing mind or that the feeling of disassociation is somehow a step in the wrong direction, can have the same effect.

If the seer can stay in this state for more than a few weeks, it becomes a way of life. The concern of loved ones who interpret the symptoms of this phase as depression, must be avoided. A month of interacting as sparingly as possible with others would help.

Phase 2. The Bliss (Transmutation). Just as surely as the seer knew that he is no-thing in the previous phase, just as surely does he now know that he is all things in this phase. It happens suddenly and begins as a blissful sensation in the cells. As one walks, it feels as though everything moves through one. Laughter diminished greatly during the first phase, but now it feels as though laughter is bubbling through the cells. The sex drive is virtually non-existent, since one cannot desire something one knows already to be part of oneself.

Just like the second phase of ego-identification, addiction is again the challenge here. At this higher level, however, few ever leave this phase. The world is accustomed to someone being 'in bliss' and frequently devotees support the physical needs of the seer at this point. To the onlooker it appears as though the master has 'arrived' and this phase seems much holier than the next one.

Although the seer in his bliss cares little for what others think, the devotees' care of him doesn't assist in awakening the desire to leave this intoxicating state. The seer has no boundaries and only allows. This leaves him wide open to others who promote his dependency on them in order to feel needed and feed their own egos. The seer will be able to see their motives clearly, but like a benign parent that laughs at a child's folly, will indulge them.

The formidable temptation the bliss presents cannot be stressed enough. Even with years of training to know there is no point of arrival, the bliss is inclined to drive the training out of one's head. During this and the previous phase, the seer withdraws from the opposition human experiences present. As a result, all growth stops since friction is necessary for progress.

Time lies around one like a spider web as linear time continues to be meaningless. The seer can see alternate futures like points on the web–the most likely future has the most threads through it. But because time lies in all directions, there is little difference between the future and the past.

Phase 3. Re-Entering the Human Condition (Transfiguration). Like a glimmer here and there, the memory stirs through the bliss reminding that there is something more; that if the seer stays in the bliss, the power he has accumulated with such effort throughout his life will sift through his fingers like sand.

As in the previous cycle's third phase, the accumulation of power in this phase is absolutely crucial to make the transition to the third and final stage of human development–Ascended Mastery. The rungs of the ladder are not evenly spaced. Breaching the gap between the three stages takes an enormous amount of energy to achieve.

The only way to accumulate power without damaging oneself or the web of existence is through gaining more perception. The seer has to re-engage in human interaction to gain the insights. If he does not, he stays polarized into the light (the known) when all new insight comes from delving into the unknown (dark).

It takes great humility and dedication to the path to leave the obvious mastery (which others recognize and support) of the bliss and blunder back into the human drama, seemingly as foolish as everyone else. But one cannot re-enter the womb any more than an adult body can become that of a child again. Thus even as we once again laugh our laughter and cry our tears, underneath the surface the vast stillness remains.

The seer, new to the human drama from the vastness of this level of perception, in fact blunders more than most. To many it may seem as though their master had feet of clay after all. True to the co-dependent triangle of most people's affections (leg one = I adore, leg two = I control, leg three = I find you to have feet of clay), their attitude becomes one of 'if you don't let me control you or you step out of the box of expectations I erected around you, I reject you'.

Three minds work simultaneously towards the end of this phase: the surface mind, 4th dimensional higher mind and the vast highest mind. If someone asks a question, three answers from all three minds' perspectives present themselves. The answer the seer gives will be gauged to the level of the recipient's ability to understand.

The way in which power tests a masterful seer at this level has seldom been revealed since few make it this far and fewer still speak about it. Circumstances respond to the seer's intent at this point. If a parking space isn't available, he can manifest circumstances that will produce one. In this way he can create less opposition in his life, but with it, less growth and accumulated power.

To his great amusement, the seer discovers that having gained enough power to change the circumstances of his life, he is unable to do so. Instead, he has become fully co-operative with life. If he has to park his car several blocks away from his destination, he does so and finds there a homeless person whom he knows he has a contract to assist.

What the seer does create at this point, however, are situations to give others the opportunity to grow. It happens effortlessly and without attachment to outcome. The seer sees the flaw, creates a 'space of expectation' in his mind (like a mold the universe rushes to fill), and the opportunity arises for the student to look his own flaw in the face.

Stage 3: Ascended Mastery

Phase 1. Original Thinking (Transformation). The vast change of entering into the stage of Ascended Mastery is accompanied by the same profound visionary experiences that occur with entry into God-consciousness. It feels as though one is melting into the heart of God.

As in both previous stages' first phases, this phase is one of emptying out. The silence within the mind during God-consciousness is broken when one has to speak or write, for instance. Now, however, even that is done without conscious thought and from a place of complete silence.

It is as though the Ascended Master is on 'auto-pilot' and any action that isn't meant to be is simply impossible to take; the hand will not dial the phone number or pick up the pen even if the reason why isn't yet clear. If there is any resistance, dishonesty or agenda, a swirling sensation takes place as though one is in a vortex of confusion.

Because surface mind is seldom used, there is a great deal of energy at one's disposal. In fact, if one refrains from reading or any activity that needs the deduction of surface mind, one can go days without sleep. Anesthetics no longer work as they block the surface mind and one doesn't often use that mind in everyday life.

The source of genius that some are privileged to feel on occasion or in a particular field, is the Ascended Master's constant companion. The mind is almost totally silent but the answer to any question is immediately there. The answers require an existing vocabulary to understand, but if one can understand the question, the answer will be given.

The miracles during this phase increase dramatically, but if they are not on the Ascended Master's path to demonstrate, they will not be done in front of others.

Phase 2. Immortality (Transmutation). This experience of a lifetime feels as though the cells 'pop' like popcorn while the body feels on fire and tingles all over. The luminous cocoon around the body doubles in size. Symptoms leading up to this experience include:

- Pressure in the back of the head where the process seems to begin;
- Light-headedness and spatial disorientation. This includes the feeling of the head 'opening' at the crown;
- Anesthetics don't work. Local anesthetics require quadruple dosages but immediately wear off (like dental injections);
- Pain is experienced differently–more like an unpleasant pressure;
- Everyone seems to be in slow motion, their thoughts disorganized and slow;
- There is the premonition that life is about to change forever.

After the event, beings of all descriptions congregate around the Immortal Master and for those who perceive energy directly, the light around the body is so dense that the features are hardly discernable. The ability to become immortal is rare among species and noteworthy enough that many unseen hands come to touch one's face.

As in the previous two stages' second phases, there is an addictive quality that must be overcome before moving on. The energy lines that twine through the chakras (in women they go sideways and in men back to front) create an endocrine secretion in the brain that generates intense bliss, less diffuse and more orgasmic than the previous stages' bliss. A sweet tasting fluid is excreted in the back of the throat. The enticement is to totally surrender to the bliss and withdraw from human interaction.

Phase 3. Ascended Master (Transfiguration). As the book goes to press I have just entered this stage and have not yet experienced its testing. From the previous stages we can deduce that its testing has something to do with the use of power. The teachings have been the result of personal revelations or experience and the readers will have to wait with me for the characteristics of this stage to reveal themselves. Hopefully the next book will be able to describe this glorious stage where all things are subject to the master who lives beyond mortal boundaries.

God is in the Pyramid

The ancient Maya called God "Hunab Ku" which translated from the original Mayan language means: God is in the Pyramid. (See Figure 9, God is in the Pyramid) The secret behind this phrase reveals the future evolution of man; what lies beyond the culmination of the human experience which is ascension.

Observing the illustration of the seven bodies of man, the

God is in the Pyramid

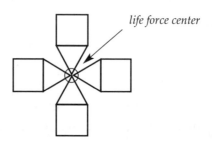

life force center

STEP 1: Mental bodies can merge. Feminine or frequency bodies don't merge but harmoniously interact. To illustrate this: Cut out the above shapes and fold as instructed in step 2.

STEP 2: When all four squares are folded over each other, they form the base. The adjoining triangles form a four-sided pyramid.

Hunab Ku

STEP 3: The lifeforce center becomes enlarged and expands to contain the pyramid within. This occurs when a human moves beyond the five stages of human evolution.

☐ = mental bodies   △ = frequency or feminine bodies   ◯ = lifeforce center or zero point

(Figure 9)

squares represent mental aspects or mind. The triangles represent emotional aspects. As we become Ascended Masters, all aspects of mind merge until eventually pure original thought (which we call genius) becomes all there is.

As we cut out the horizontal and the vertical axis as illustrated, we can therefore merge all the squares by gluing them one on top of the other. We then find that the emotional aspects, the triangles, pop upwards and form the four sides of a pyramid. They, unlike the mental aspects, do not merge, but harmoniously interact like four notes forming a chord.

When we observe the relationships inherent in the four-sided pyramid, we can interpret it in our own lives in two ways. Firstly, within man there are eight basic emotions, represented by four sides each having a positive and negative pole. When those eight emotions are brought into harmony, it enables our minds to merge into the stages of Ascended Mastery and beyond.

Secondly, as the minds merge and the emotions become harmonious and balanced, the seven bodies of man assume the same relationships as depicted by the pyramid. The life force center enlarges and encloses the pyramid and instead of the luminous cocoon of man, the spherical life-force centre surrounds the body. The stage beyond Ascended Master is the God Kingdom. A god-being has a self-sustaining life-force sphere in which it dwells. With our field forming such a vehicle we can travel through time and space with the speed of thought to explore the cosmos. The god-being is in the pyramid.

On a practical level, an incredibly profound truth is revealed by the relationships of the triangles or sides of the pyramid: all emotions, even the seemingly negative ones of anger, fear, and pain have equal value within the evolution of man. Virtually all spiritual teachings of the world have overlooked this truth and have favored joy as valuable, anger as unacceptable, fear as either undesirable or of less value and pain as something to be overcome or endured.

1. **Joy/Passion** When joy (negative pole) is not alternating with its positive pole, it can become self-centeredness. When passion (positive pole) is not balanced with joy, it can become aggression. For joy and passion to be in balance, both poles (which yield each other alternately) must express in equal measure.

2. **Anger/Protectiveness** (positive pole) is the desire to attack or break up. When not balanced by the desire to protect (negative pole), it can become rage, and when rage is not allowed to express, depression (the desire to self-destruct). When it is in balance it attacks that which is stuck or suppresses light. When anger expresses, it is often indiscriminately directed at the situation in front of it. Only afterwards can we see which pieces of the illusion have now dissipated. Protectiveness, on the other hand, has identified what is worth fighting for. Once again these opposite poles yield each other.

3. **Fear/Love** Fear (negative pole) shrinks from certain aspects of life, which could serve as a warning that we have encountered something we are not yet prepared to handle. We can either accept the challenge and increase our skill level in that specific area, or realize that we cannot yet step up to that particular challenge and retreat. Either way it reveals areas where self-improvement is needed. It also reveals the parts of life we haven't yet embraced in compassionate understanding. The positive pole is love, which is the desire to include. When fear is suppressed and it doesn't serve to help us expand our love, our love becomes exclusive, loving only that which we can relate to.

4. **Pain/Contentment** When positively expressed, pain is the

divine discontent that leads us to seek a better way, a higher road, a way out, or a way forward. The opposite pole of pain is contentment–the desire to retain or keep. It is the feeling of having arrived at the right place or having found the right thing; of living a perfect moment. Pain arises from something needing to change; contentment stems from a feeling of being filled and having our needs met.

Emotions are like pulsating colors, from the higher range of the spectrum such as the violets (the negative poles of the emotions) to the lower range of reds and oranges (the positive poles of the emotions). The sides of the pyramidal field are therefore pulsating colors, surrounded by the enlarged lifeforce center sphere around it in white light. This is the exquisite field of a god-being.

Preparing the Body for Increased Light

Discomfort can occur in the body as the cells fill with light from increased perception. Increased light can cause a very unpleasant burning sensation in the limbs if the body's acidity levels are too high. Furthermore, light seekers often experience feelings of spaciness as they are unable to ground their enhanced states of consciousness. This may be alleviated by the use of trace minerals, no longer commonly found in our soil. They therefore need to be nutritionally supplemented.

Increased meditative states flush toxins out of the liver. The body will also shed its toxicity automatically when major transformations happen. Increased light requires a certain physical purity and will shed the toxicity until that level of purity is reached. This happens very noticeably when you enter God-consciousness and even more so when you enter the Ascended Master stage as layers of toxicity found in mortality are shed. Preparations for increased light within the physical could smooth the way and help facilitate these changes.

The Seven Bands of Nutrition

The nutrients needed by the body not only nourish the physical body but establish links between all seven bodies. The seven bodies of man represent the seven levels of light and frequency within Creation. Each level of light carries information received by one of the endocrine glands.

An octave of frequency separates one body from another. In the same way, an octave of frequency separates the frequency bands of nutrition from one another. Each band has a very different function and a unique way of behaving. (<u>See Figure 10, The Seven Bands of Nutrition</u>)

The First Band of Nutrition

These minerals are involved in cell formation, the building and maintenance of bones, blood, and the smooth working of muscles and other soft tissue functions. They include iron, magnesium, calcium, zinc, and others. These minerals work with the autonomic or self–regulatory nervous system.

The Second Band of Nutrition:

The second band works with frequencies that permeate the body. They are what scientists call reflective and include nickel, silver, and chromium. They are necessary for protein assimilation, fat and sugar metabolism. They feed the autonomic nervous system and assist with fruitful dreaming and the ability to work out existing karma painlessly by being able to 'see' the subtle information that we refer to as insights.

The Seven Bands of Nutrition

BAND OF NUTRITION	CLEARS	EXAMPLE
1st Band: The basic building blocks for bones, blood and other tissues that work with the autonomic nervous system.	Physical body's channels	calcium, iron, magnesium, zinc
2nd Band: These reflective minerals regulate the bodily functions through frequency. They work with fat and sugar assimilation. They feed the autonomic nervous system.	Etheric body's channels	nickel, silver, chromium, phosphorous
3rd Band: Regulate the body's hormones. These trace minerals feed the parasympathetic nervous system. Brings emotional well-being.	Emotional body's channels	vanadium, gold, titanium
4th Band: These Electrical Precursor Energies (EPC's) stimulate the higher hormones that are responsible for the transfiguration of the body.	Mental body's channels	EPC's are found in negative ions in nature, sounds generated by nature, EPC devices such as pyramids and crystals lit with lasers.
5th Band: Sound healing through our own voices and the frequencies of the ascension attitudes: love, praise and gratitude. It opens the endocrine system's hidden fourth dimensional qualities.	Promotes access to Spiritual-Emotional body	Aligning with seasonal frequencies. Receiving or giving love and also from to the earth's frequencies
6th Band: Light healing through the colors of nature and through recapitulation which allows the light from the spiritual-mental body to penetrate through to the physical body.	Promotes access to Spiritual-Mental body	The blue sky without pollution or obstruction by glasses. The greenery of nature
7th Band: Brings in the third type of awareness: Original Awareness. Prepares the human through the endocrine system for the evolutionary stages beyond humanness. Enlarges the lifeforce center.	Clears the pollution from the light-fibers of the Spirit Body	Clearing lightfibers by eliminating conditioning from external sources. Geopathic anti-stress devises help clear these nutritional pathways.

(Figure 10)

85

The Third Band of Nutrition:

These minerals, called trace minerals, are no longer available in the soil and must be supplemented until the body becomes completely self-sustaining in the later phases of the 3rd stage of human evolution. These minerals like vanadium, gold, and titanium ensure the smooth functioning of the parasympathetic nervous system. They work with the body's hormones to produce emotional stability and a sense of well-being. They are essential for the promptings, information, and energy that come through the emotional body from the three highest spiritual bodies.

The Fourth Band of Nutrition:

In his book *"Rays of Truth Crystals of Light"* Dr. Fred Bell, Former NASA scientist, writes: "Electrical Precursation (EPC) is the energy that in the end controls the consciousness of all individual cells. It has basic polarities in that electrical precursation is either stressful or healing. The body, although biochemical in its nature, is also electrical. Electricity controls each and every step of our cellular and organism growth."

Dr. Bell explains that cell reproduction starts in the DNA where tiny "command signals called Electrical Precursor Energies (EPC's)" are interpreted. This in turn stimulates the body's super–hormones. "…subtle forces such as EPC's can no longer be regarded as subtle, but instead, should be recognized as being of the same magnitude as what we eat, drink, and breathe into our bodies!"

The primary sources for EPC's are: (1) negative ions found in nature or ion generators; (2) Sounds generated by nature; (3) Electrical Precursation devices such as pyramids and crystals.

The Fourth Band Of Nutrition, consisting of EPC's in the proper polarity, allows enhanced perception to occur and establishes subtle pathways to the mental body from the physical body. Enhanced perception yields energy, which yields power used to regenerate cells.

EPC's allow the thymus to interpret the feelings, (non-cognitive ways of receiving information), generated by the information brought back from the body's cells through the venous system. The blood returning to the heart is laden with the information deposited at the cellular level and received from the tiny 'commands signals' (EPC's).

The Fifth Band of Nutrition:

The fifth band of nutrition consists of pure frequency or sound. Much information on sound healing is available and the volume grows annually. The portions that are not as widely understood concern the more subtle frequencies unheard by the human ear:

• Frequency varies with the time of day. There are optimum times during which to treat certain conditions. This can be tested by dividing the day into segments of 2 hours each. Touching the body over the origin of the disease and muscle testing for the strongest time of the day provides the primary time for focusing healing. To gather meticulous data small weights may have to be used.

• The frequencies of the seasons are beneficial to some bodily systems while others manifest disease during some parts of the year if the individual is out of synchronicity with the frequency. An example would be: in the month of October the energies in nature move inward in the Northern Hemisphere. Plants withdraw their sap and their life force from their outer extremities (such as the leaves) to their inner (the roots). Energy in nature becomes more magnetic (earth) than electric (sun) and withdraws into the earth.

Humans that do not co-operate with this cycle by stilling outer activity and taking time for inner feelings (if one becomes sensitive to these feelings one can feel the seasons change within), are prone to develop respiratory diseases. Oriental medicine practitioners take these seasonal frequencies into consideration.

- The earth's frequency has the ability to give health to the lower glands of the endocrine system. Wearing earth resonant shoes when walking on earth allows us to absorb these delicate frequencies. The rubber soles of most shoes act as insulators and cut us off from these health promoting frequencies. We should have a life style that permits the assimilation of these frequencies by walking or standing on earth at least 40-60 minutes a day.

- When we resist life, or when we are in a rut, we lose some resonant frequencies in our voice. Our own voice is a tremendous sound healing device and the reduction of frequency will manifest in diminished health. New activities and experiences provide one way of restoring the frequencies and will be felt as increased energy in the body.

- Stuck patterns in the body can be broken up not only by the use of rattles or the recorded sound of thunder, but by the frequency of love and appreciation being directed at the specific area. Memories of abuse or trauma held in such a stuck pattern can be released this way.

- The greatest healing frequencies of all are the ascension attitudes of love, praise, and gratitude that not only have the capability of healing the cells, but to spiritualize them in such a way that it can change the body from mortal to immortal. In other words, frequency as a healing tool also activates the ability of the spiritual-emotional body to change the 'unreal' or transient into the 'real' or spiritualized matter.

The Sixth Band of Nutrition:

- This source of nutrition and health for the body is what is com-

monly referred to as light therapy. The pollution above cities, fil-
tration by window panes, sunglasses, glasses and contact lenses
all prevent some of the shorter rays (the indigo, blue and green
rays) from penetrating the eye fully. This adversely effects the
functioning of the upper endocrine system.

- The lack of greenery in the concrete jungles where many of us
  work and live impairs the functioning of the immune system.
  The colors found in nature are balanced for the energies of specific geographical locations to produce health. It will be found
  that people gravitating to certain terrains have auras deficient in
  those colors found in that area. When someone lives in an environment that balances out colors lacking in their aura, that person feels healthy, balanced, and strong. The same principle
  applies in the choice of clothing. For instance, the corporate
  world is a very stressful environment that causes adrenal over-
  load and deficiencies in the kidneys. Black balances this out and
  is predominantly worn in business environments.

- The essential skill of recapitulation or gaining insights from past
  experiences yields perception; in other words it turns the
  unknown (un-accessed light) into the known (accessed light).
  This increases the light permeating the lower four bodies.
  Eventually the mental body becomes so balanced and still that it
  opens up to guidance from the higher spiritual-mental body
  (God-consciousness). When this refined light floods the five
  lower bodies, it not only changes the cells to immortal, but sets
  humankind free from all mortal boundaries. It lifts a God-conscious being (stage 2) into an Immortal Master (stage 3) and
  makes the advanced phases of stage 3 available in which the
  body no longer needs to eat since it has become self-sustaining,
  or fed by light.

The Seventh Band of Nutrition:

The seventh band of nutrition has its source within the fields of the human body: the life force center located within the midriff section of the body, appearing as a ball of white light about the size of a grapefruit. In Ascended Masters, however, it becomes large enough during the final phase to envelop all seven bodies and feed them self-sustaining life force.

The seventh band of nutrition brings 'on line' the light fibers in the spirit body of man. This body consists of trillions and trillions of light fibers radiating out from the life force center behind the belly-button through all the other bodies, ending in the luminous cocoon of man. The light fibers are representative of all life that exists within All That Is (all seven bodies of the Infinite).

The ability for man to move beyond the three developmental stages of his evolution of awareness (there is never a point of arrival and there is always a potential waiting to become), lies within this body. When the three stages of development have been completed and the body is spiritualized and immortal, this band supplies the frequencies of all other nutritional bands and even breathing becomes obsolete.

The vitality and wholeness the life force center can provide to all bodies can be disrupted when there is pollution in the fibers. Pollution is the direct result of outside programming imposed on an individual.

- The primary form of mind-control we are subjected to is social conditioning. This includes deliberate parental and educational conditioning, the slanted world views produced by un-recapitulated events, the personal identity we give ourselves and are given by outside mirrors.
- The technological tools used through television, some movies,

some DVD's and beamed directly at geographical areas are mass mind control programs. These could effect our light fibers unless we are aware enough and clear enough to recognize that the feelings of fear, rage, grief or lust are not our own and refuse to accept them.

When the pollution in the light fibers is cleared away and the energy that was tied up in holding the pollution in place becomes available to the seven bodies, the life force center grows larger and the light fibers come 'on line' (they light up). The life force center eventually becomes so enlarged that it forms a ball of light that encompasses all seven bodies and the light fibers start to receive energy from the light fibers of the macro-cosmos. As the human being transfigures into the stages that lie beyond those discussed in this book, he moves all Creation, which is now connected through the activated light fibers having come on line, up with him.

Stages Of Sexual Development

Understanding the four bands of compassion found within the Infinite and its Creation is a bit like discovering the Fibonacci sequence for the first time. Once you know it, it suddenly becomes apparent in life's expressions all around you. The four bands of compassion will be found to provide the pattern for evolving life everywhere, from conflict resolution, social and relationship stages to sexual development. (See Figure 11, Four Great Bands of Compassion)

The sexual stages of man pertain to the way the opposite sexes relate to one another and move through the bands of compassion from the top (as illustrated) to the bottom during identity consciousness. Immediately preceding God-consciousness they begin moving from the bottom to the top, symbolizing the blue road home.

Four Great Bands of Compassion

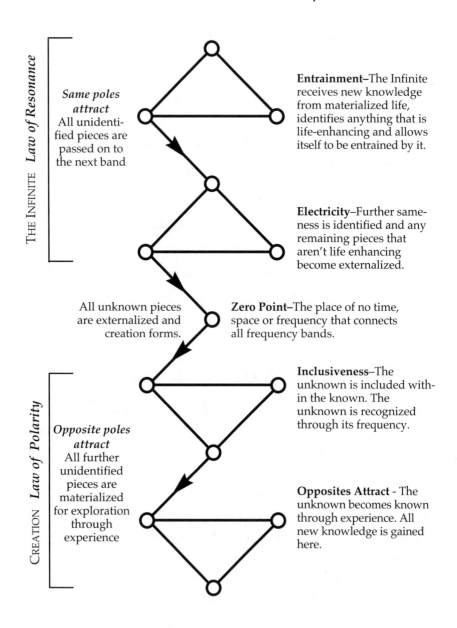

THE INFINITE *Law of Resonance*

Same poles attract
All unidentified pieces are passed on to the next band

Entrainment–The Infinite receives new knowledge from materialized life, identifies anything that is life-enhancing and allows itself to be entrained by it.

Electricity–Further sameness is identified and any remaining pieces that aren't life enhancing become externalized.

All unknown pieces are externalized and creation forms.

Zero Point–The place of no time, space or frequency that connects all frequency bands.

Inclusiveness–The unknown is included within the known. The unknown is recognized through its frequency.

CREATION *Law of Polarity*

Opposite poles attract
All further unidentified pieces are materialized for exploration through experience

Opposites Attract - The unknown becomes known through experience. All new knowledge is gained here.

These four frequency bands form the matrix offer all evolving life. By aligning with them, we draw upon the power of the All.

(Figure 11)

In the current industrialized societies these natural developmental stages have been severely disrupted through corruption from the media, the increase of neglect and child abuse resulting from the destruction of primary family units. When societies are declining or de-structuring, this becomes the case. Traditional stages of sexual development occur in the following sequence: (See Figure 12, Sexual Stages of Mankind)

1. Seeking Sameness: (Pre-adolescence)

During pre-adolescence boys and girls gravitate towards same sex groups in order to learn more about what it means to be a boy or a girl by observing it in their same sex peers. Boys build "Keep Girls Out" clubhouses and girls often view boys as the 'enemy' as they huddle together in giggling groups. If sexual activity does occur, it usually involves same sex masturbation or exploration of the self through self-masturbation.

2. Seeking Sameness With Interest in the Opposite: (Adolescence)

While still staying in the safety of the same sex peer groups, adolescents now develop an obsessive interest in the opposite sex. During this stage the quest to understand their own sexuality continues but with increasing curiosity about the opposite sex.

Boys spend hours lifting weights, considering cars to drive when they get old enough to have a license and other 'manly' pursuits that are culturally appropriate. It is a time of proving themselves as 'a man'. Hours are spent studying and obsessively speculating about the opposite sex.

Girls spend a great deal of time with their same sex peers learning to become 'a woman'. They study magazines, makeup, and fashion. They worry endlessly about their bodies and appearance, fed by the unrealistic portrayal of the feminine ideal the media gives. They speculate in groups about the opposite sex. Generally,

Sexual Stages of Mankind

4. Seeking Only Sameness– During the final stage of human evolution, one only identifies with indwelling life and not form. Another is seen as a door to eternity..

1. Seeking Sameness– Pre-adolescence. Boys and girls seek same sex playmates. This strengthens sexual identity.

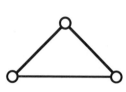

3. Examining Humanness within Oneness– We re-enter the human condition even though we remember our oneness. If it is conducive to growth, we may choose to engage in sex.

2. Seeking Sameness *(with intense interest in opposite sex)*– Early-adolescence. Boys and girls each participate in same sex activities but obsess about the opposite sex.

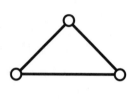

2. All is Experienced Within *(first two phases of God consciousness)*– We live total inclusiveness. It is impossible to desire another.

3. Understanding the Opposite *(by experiencing it within the familiar)*– Late teens and early twenties. Boys and girls experience the opposite sex within groups of combined sexes. The relationships are more superficial.

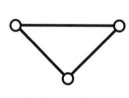

1. Opposites Merge *(preceding entry into God consciousness)*– The masculine and feminine within merge to give birth to the God-being. Sexual desires decline.

4. Experiencing the Opposite– Mid twenties and later. In-depth and isolated relationships form with mental/emotional exploration. We get to know our own opposite sex within by studying it in another.

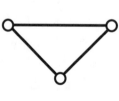

GOD-CONSCIOUSNESS *(Stages evolve this way)*

IDENTITY CONSCIOUSNESS *(Stages evolve this way)*

Understanding these stages can aid us in honoring where we and others are along the path of unfoldment in human sexuality.

(Figure 12)

94

if sex does occur with the opposite sex, they retreat back into the same sex group as their main support group after the encounter.

3. Understanding the Opposite by Experiencing it Within the Familiar: (Late teens, early twenties)

Cliques or groups of both sexes with similar interests form so that they may study each other in the safety of the group. Sororities, the 'jocks' and cheerleaders, the intellectuals, the rebels and other groups with similar characteristics form.

Sexual encounters can now be explored with one another within the safety of a support group with similar values. At a time when they are still unsure about their sexuality, their peers mirror to them that they are acceptable through their sameness (unfortunately a similar reason forms the basis of many friendships, locking people into approved stagnation).

The sexual relationships are superficial during this stage. They are not interested in the deep exploration of the emotions or minds of their partners but rather in broadening their experience.

4. Experiencing the Opposite: (Mid-twenties and later)

During the mid-twenties and later, isolated relationships form and the association with peer groups becomes more peripheral. The opposite sex is now studied in depth as we search to understand our own inner opposite gender through our partners. The emotions and thoughts of partners become as important as the physical aspects of the relationship.

Sex And God-consciousness

When we enter advanced stages of spiritual evolution, sexuality changes yet again. The changes mirror the bands of compassion in reverse order (from the bottom to the top). (See Figure 13, Developmental Stages of Compassion) The sexual stages within

The Developmental Stages of Compassion

4. We engineer teaching experiences for others. We remain incapable of supporting human folly unless it evolves awareness

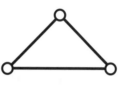

1. Feeling compassion for those we identify with, namely, our tribe, race, nation, etc.

3. We start to practice a form of tough love. Our compassion supports only indwelling life and we withdraw any support that keeps another in illusion

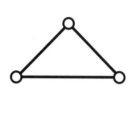

2. Feeling compassion for those we identify with and outsiders who have the same traits or adopt our sameness

2. We continue to see the value of all life, but it floods our being to such an extent that we only allow. We have embraced all within our inclusiveness

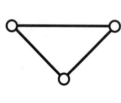

3. Feeling compassion for those who are different, but want to convert them to that which we represent

1. Just prior to entering God consciousness, we start to see the value of those who play opposite roles and grateful compassion comes into being

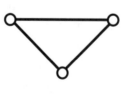

4. Feeling compassion for those who are different, but we still want to 'save' those we judge as less fortunate

Understanding these stages can aid us to overcome the tendency of one stage to judge another as lacking in compassion. We can clearly see how the level of perception determines the level of compassion.

(Figure 13)

God-consciousness move through the bands of compassion from the lower frequencies to the highest; in the opposite direction and at a higher level than the stages of someone in identity consciousness.

1. Opposites Merge: (Preceding entry into God-consciousness)

One of the pre-requisites to entering God-consciousness is that the masculine and feminine within each person come into perfect balance. The inner union of the masculine and feminine dramatically reduces the sexual desire for another. The ability to fall in love is only present when there is an imbalance between our own inner masculine and feminine.

2. All is Experienced Within: (The first two phases of God-consciousness)

To be in God-consciousness is a change so dramatic that one still in identity consciousness can only speculate about it. The idea of having sex with another when first there is no self and then, in the second phase, there is no other, becomes nonsensical. The bliss of the second phase is far more intense than a physical orgasm and the physical aspects of life lose their appeal. The sex drive becomes non-existent.

The God-conscious person who is in a relationship may continue sexual activity with a partner however, simply because he or she only allows during these stages. There are no boundaries to one who has seen his or her true identity during these first two phases.

3. Examining Humanness Within Oneness: (Re-entering the human condition)

Re-entering the human condition while remembering our larger identity, we again act as though we are separate from others in order to grow. If it is conducive to evolving the awareness of ourselves and others, we may choose to re-engage in sex.

Because a master at this level serves only the purposes of indwelling life, sex will be the result of inner guidance received through the heart and not because of physical needs. Once the decision has been made to have sex, the master's focus contracts to the physical in order to enjoy the experience.

4. Seeking Only Sameness: (The Ascended Master)

At this point the master only engages in sacred sex, if at all. He sees another as part of himself but now also clearly sees how unique the perspective is that each person has of life. He may therefore direct his universal love temporarily toward another and enter his partner as though through a door to enjoy the partner's unique eternal perspective. From this experience the master's own perspective gains enrichment.

Discovering Our Destiny

To understand the meaning of destiny, we have to understand our relationship with the Infinite. At what point did we individuate into a multitude of perspectives, each one a unique facet of the Infinite?

Think of the initial explosion–the Big Bang–as a spreading of sticky glue all over a spider web as vast as the space that defines where Creation will take place. The spider sitting in the middle of the spider web will now get caught in her own web's glue, so she plucks the strands of her web the way a harpist plucks the strings of her harp. As she does so, the glue clusters into droplets. She can now run between them on her dainty feet to retrieve her food without getting caught herself.

Frequency or vibration causes the clustering of energy into matter, just like the spider's glue. If we place a circle of thick paper covered with metal shavings on top of a glass and strike a tuning fork against the glass, different patterns will form for different notes

The harpist or the tuning fork that clusters awareness into individuated perspectives is the desire (frequency) of the Infinite to know itself through forming Creation. From this clustering, each one of us becomes a unique facet of the Infinite, able to relate to one another and to plan the way we want Creation to unfold.

This individuation takes place before the Infinite divides itself into Creator and Creation. To further understand how we relate to the Infinite at this point, we have to look at the sub-personalities within man: the inner nurturer, the inner child, the inner warrior, and the inner sage. The sub-personalities are not outside ourselves, nor separate from ourselves. Each one is a specific and unique perspective superimposed over our inner space or psyche, able to converse with one another.

The unique perspective each one of us has, carries with it a unique challenge which becomes our destiny. Each one of us receives a part of the mathematical equation that is the Infinite to explore as part of our solving the mystery of beingness. For example: $(a+b) + (x-y) + (qr-s) = $ The Infinite

In other words, when Creation is formed, Jane will design life–time after life-time exploring issues around $(a+b)$, John will explore $(x-y)$ and so forth. The part of the equation of the Infinite's being we undertake to solve becomes our destiny.

Let us take a look at the way destiny unfolds in the case of Jane. Something still to be solved is part of illusion or the unknown. Let us therefore choose a subject such as suffering as her destiny to understand.

Jane is as yet a specific awareness of consciousness, individuated through the desire of the Infinite. When Creation, the mirror image of the Infinite forms, it mirrors Jane's individuation back to her. At the higher level of Creation, what we call her higher self will form. At the lower level of Creation her higher self will interpret her highest self's destiny, and create various lifetimes within manifestation (form) to explore this destiny through experience.

The letter "a" in her theme is suffering. She lives lifetimes such as:

$$Suffering + rescuing = dependency$$
$$Or$$
$$Suffering + perception = power$$

We call a specific life's contribution to understanding the destiny, fate. Our fate (the themes we are trying to understand in this life) is but one step in a line of many. How much of our destiny line can we find? Can we unravel the mysteries shrouding that moment when the One became many and we covenanted with the Infinite and all other creations to undertake with dedication and valor the exploring of our part of the equation? We pledged that we would turn darkness to light enriching the whole with our insights. How can we find what it was we contracted to do?

To pierce the mists that veil the large theme our experiences are shedding light on is an enormously important endeavor. Not only does it heal our wounds by putting our suffering into perspective, but it provides us with a powerful tool that yields further enlightenment: inclusiveness.

In a nutshell, inclusiveness is the compassionate understanding of the large picture. The larger the part of Creation we can embrace and see the absolute perfection of, the more power at our disposal to help us gain further insights and perception. To help us understand inclusiveness further, we examine the difference between an archangel and a nature deva.

The nature deva overseeing the creation of a rosebush and the archangel Mi-ka-el overseeing the stepping down of light into matter are both equally important to the Infinite in that each one is a strand in the great web of life. If either were to be removed the perfection of the whole would cease to be. If Creation mirrors the Infinite, Mi-ka-el holds a larger part of the mirror which yields vast power and the little nature deva holds but a sliver mirroring a smaller part of the Infinite's reflection.

Our collective lifetimes are like a large inclusive mirror that has shattered into many little pieces, reflecting individual lives. Through retrieving the insights of these lives we can piece the big mirror back together. We begin by finding the themes in this lifetime that are either predominant or recurring.

Life's themes often occur in cycles, the most notable being those of seven and twenty-one years. Themes are subtle at times, but once found, reveal themselves in layers. For instance, at first it may appear the theme is debilitating suffering, but as we look further we realize that the 'damaged' areas of our lives can become our strong suits. They are sources of great power if we can turn them around by gaining their insights and adjusting our attitudes from feeling victimized to embracing our experiences in the knowledge that our higher selves wrote the script. The theme could therefore be that suffering could lead to insights and power.

Then we realize that much of our suffering came as a result of our resistance to change and that suffering is but the tool of awareness to force change. In this way the theme could be explored, like peeling an onion, until the core stands revealed. It could be, for example, that suffering occurs when we believe form to be real instead of indwelling life and that by changing our focus to indwelling life we can flourish in the midst of suffering.

Using past life regression therapy, we follow the themes we have thoroughly explored for insights in this life. We follow not only the themes, but lives we have lived with the key players in these events. At times we need to go back many times to a particular life to fully understand the insights it yields. We may have to be prepared to find those lives on other planets and most importantly, also in the future.[6] As we trace back the lives we have shared with the key players in our present life, we may find that we have many times reversed roles. Eventually our tracks through time will lead to pure, formless awareness where we contracted with one another to provide the necessary friction to promote growth. Perhaps we may even see how great the compassion and inclusiveness must have been for others to play roles contrary to the light that they are, just so that we may fulfill our destiny in the most glorious way possible.

Once we uncover our destiny, the nature of our challenges change. No longer do we go around on a treadmill of unlearned lessons, but instead, the challenges become relevant to our destiny. We then find the same satisfaction from meeting these challenges as would a mountain climber who, with each overcoming watches with satisfaction as he slowly but surely approaches his goal: a view that seems to stretch into eternity with a blinding beauty that takes the breath away.

The Three Ascension Attitudes

The attitudes of love, praise, and gratitude are representative of the trinity found throughout the matrix of existence. They are the crowning glory of a sanctified life. They are the vehicle to the immortality and ascension that await man beyond his present horizon.

Love

Emerson wrote:

> *"Alas! I know not why... each man sees over his own experience a certain stain of error, whilst that of other men looks fair and ideal."*

6 Readers are referred to recorded material on *Painless Past Life Regression*, part 3.

The reason we look back with so much regret at what we regard as our folly, is that the memory of our higher levels of consciousness lies not far submerged beneath the surface of mind. We suppress with pain the memory of the faces we once loved, and guilt taints many of the choices we have made in our lives.

We dishonor the journey of our lives, however, by not acknowledging the worth of our seeming errors as our great teachers of wisdom. Remove one failed relationship or one foolish choice, and one would also have to remove as much wisdom and insight. Nowhere does the sting of self-censure torture us more than in the memories of love lost or misplaced.

The word love is bandied about from pulpits, across restaurant tables, in flowery cards of all descriptions. The fact is that very few philosophers have shed much light on how the love we feel in romance and the love for God and Creation can be reconciled. Romantic love is either extolled in the very abundant sources of literature or the more spiritual writings dismiss it as an unworthy reflection of infinite love.

The result is that because romantic love is the most intoxicating feeling most humans will ever have (called by philosophers "the enchantment of human life"), the guilt is compounded by feeling that such intense love should instead have been given to God. In the lives of most, no love will ever again compare to the heady, runaway, romantic emotion of youth. Thus we find ourselves lacking in devotion and so try to love God with all the fervor we can muster, to most a nebulous and undefined concept. This often creates religious fanatics who, failing in their feelings, try to compensate through their actions.

It is the very turbulence of our romantic love that carves out of our souls the hollows that will hold a greater love. It is through our love for a lover, a father, a mother, a child that our love grows to include all people. Like the stormiest seas carving the deepest caverns in the cliffs, so too the most painful memories create our deepest capacity for love.

My mother spent her last years in an old age home in a little town 15 hours by car from where I live. I tried to have her moved to where our family could give her attention and care, but the doctors felt she might suffer a fatal heart attack from the stress of the move. The difficulty in reaching her (she later could no longer remember us when we phoned), had her die miles from her loved ones, surrounded by strangers. The pain and guilt of feeling I had failed her arose unbidden within my heart for many years. It has deepened my ability to love older people and constant silent blessings and healings flow from me when I encounter an older person and know they're someone's mother or father.

Thus very intense romantic love awakens within us the ability to love others more deeply, but it also awakens so much more. The depth an artist brings to art likewise stems from passion inspired by love. Eventually, not only that which we create but that which we are, gets honed and shaped into a maturity that is lacking in those who have never relinquished the love of self for love of another.

So we learn through our earthly loves how to surrender to something greater, that one day we may merge with our own higher identity. We find through love's muse the poet within us, the spontaneity of the inner child. We remember once again what it is like to follow our hearts and abandon reason. Love mellows us and reduces our resistance to life, and as we grow older what we forfeit in intensity we gain in inclusiveness.

The qualities of inclusiveness and surrender prepare us for God-consciousness, and here we encounter the silence of the mind. The heart cannot fully love while there is an internal dialogue, though one can only know that retrospectively. As the mind silences, the heart bursts open with an all-encompassing melting tenderness for all life. Divine love has taken its place upon the throne of the heart.

Praise

As a child, I had a fear of heights. When on the high rides of the carnival or perched in our mulberry tree, I found that I could overcome it by focusing on the far horizon. By slightly altering the focus of my eyes, the dizzy heights became friendlier.

Praise is an attitude that focuses on the distant vistas and allows itself to enjoy the breathtaking view. It acknowledges that there is an unpaid bill, but focuses instead on the nurturing and abundant supply that flows to one who trusts in it. It does not disassociate from the cares of today, but rather sees them in their true context as harbingers of growth.

Praise is an attitude of thoughts raised heavenward, nowhere better illustrated than the story of Christ walking on the water as told in the New Testament. He did not focus on the stormy seas, but steadfastly kept his focus on indwelling life rather than form. The disciple Peter on the other hand, who wished to walk on the water also, saw the billowing waves and the high winds and sank beneath the water. The master had to reach forth his hand and save him. The Christ lived in a state of praise, Peter did not.

States of praise have been employed for eons by those made holy by association. As an ascension attitude, it needs to be tempered by experience. It is not enough to withdraw from life to spend our days singing songs of praise to God. We are here first and foremost to explore the unknown and any attempt at escaping what we have undertaken to do, carries with it a penalty. To shirk our duty and highest calling in favor of retreating into ecstatic states of praise yields a form of praise that is not tested and strong.

That which has been sheltered is seldom robust, for it has not been honed by experience nor polished to a high luster by adversity. It is easy to feel praise in the hallowed sanctuary, but can we find the perfection hidden behind the appearances in the time-ravaged faces of the beggars lining a city street?

There is no redundancy in the cosmos. If there is a beggar in the street, there is also the need for him to be there. Is it the result of his consistently avoiding his next step that such painful forced change is his lot, or is it perhaps that he is solving a profound portion of the mystery of beingness that requires such a drastic mirror of that which God is not? It could be that a great master has undertaken to play this role to either shed light where there is despair or to give us the opportunity for compassionate understanding. Whatever the reason may be, there will be ample cause for praise if we change our focus from appearances to indwelling life.

Praise fills the cells with light and our footsteps become a blessing to the earth. All life we touch responds with increased growth to such a life affirming frequency. Filled with praise, we also become filled with increased light and life force, and then in the twinkling of an eye, the lightning flash of immortality changes us into an Ascended Master.

Gratitude

If true happiness lies in being happy with what we have, rather than being happy when we get what we want, gratitude is the key to happiness. It helps us value the little joys of the moment rather than wait for the large windfalls, and in doing so we learn to appreciate life.

Life consists of the small treasures like the quiet oasis of the undisturbed moment with a cup of tea that allows us to return to the inner world of contemplation. Life is the succession of the footsteps of time for us to make of them what we will. We can either turn them into the weary tread of drudgery or lighten their gait with gratitude. The cherishing warmth of a favorite quilt on a dark, rain drenched night; the moment of feeling the coming of spring in the air; the rosy cheeked pleasure of rocking a little child to sleep, eyelids weighted by the adventures of her day; all these treasured moments through awareness become ample reason for a heart to brim with gratitude.

Not only does gratitude bless us with joy, but also with increase. One of the most concealed laws of supply is that gratitude opens the floodgates of heaven, increasing anything it focuses on. Would we wish to increase our health, our abundance, and our abilities? Then the place to begin is in grateful acknowledgement of whatever allotted portions we already have. Instead of seeing how small the supply is, let us focus in appreciation and joy on how much it means to have it. With each dollar we spend with sincere, heartfelt gratitude, many more will find their way into our pocket.

Like the other ascension attitudes, gratitude is life affirming to all who come in contact with it. Indigenous peoples have always known that nature responds favorably to gratitude; that species thrive and evolve under the grateful recognition of man. Gratitude sanctifies not only the giver, but also the recipient.

The true testing of a grateful heart is found in the challenges life brings. Inclusiveness demands that gratitude, like the sun or the life giving rain, not deem one as worthy and another as not, but shed its radiance on pain and pleasure alike. It takes in-depth insight to probe behind the appearances and extract the eternal truth that God sends nothing but goodness. He sends gifts or challenges, but challenges are themselves gifts in disguise and worthy of gratitude. When this principle is applied, it soon becomes apparent that the faintest glimmer of gratitude from the heart begins to unravel the illusion concealing the gift of insight challenges hold.

If we can master the ability to be grateful in all circumstances the transfiguring power of gratitude will shine forth, changing the cells of the body into spiritualized matter. And so we become what humankind is meant to be: Ascended Masters.

The Seven Supporting Attitudes

The seven supporting attitudes as an active part in someone's life, create a person who has mastered him or herself. No longer can such a one be pulled out of the center of his or her circle by the occurrences of daily life. Such a master welcomes pain as well as joy, and sees in pain but another opportunity to triumph over resistance to life; to relinquish the desires of the ego upon the altar of indwelling life while affirming: "Thy will be done."

Running throughout these supporting attitudes is the golden thread of deep, abiding respect for the divinity within all life. They harbor respect for our own inner guidance, for time, for the mixture of folly and wisdom that belies the greater destiny of our fellow man. They bring a respect for the process of life unfolding that demands that we live life well. (See Figure 14, The Supporting Attitudes and DNA)

Time

The largest draw-bridge imaginable still rotates on the smallest fulcrum point. The tapestry of illusion spanning the vastness of the denser realms of Creation begins to unravel when a single thread is cut. The difference a single life can make in the grand scheme of

The Supporting Attitudes and DNA

**The activation of human DNA through the
ascension and supporting attitudes**

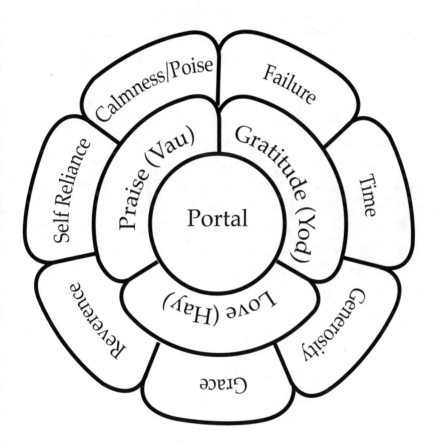

The three primary ascension attitudes and supporting attitudes that activate
chambers within the DNA after we integrate the goddess archetypes into
our lives. This results in the activation of the inner circle which is a portal to
higher consciousness through our DNA.

(Figure 14)

109

Creation is incalculably immense.

Our lives themselves hinge on the moment. One key event or insight can alter the course of a life forever, pivoting destiny in an entirely different direction. With it the outcome of events in the cosmos could pivot also. Only the most profane and shallow minded person can treat the importance of the moment as anything less than sacred.

If, for just this moment, we can see ourselves as being the center of the cosmos; as having the ability to influence with the quality of our thoughts the very fabric of existence, what would we contribute? Would it be enthusiasm and passion for the myriad of life forms that flow forth in a river of change, unstoppable in their quest to explore the unknown? Would we radiate awe and reverence for the courage of our fellow man to descend into realms of forgetfulness where pain is often our only source of guidance?

If we can see ourselves as this central point of influence, affecting all of existence, for even one second, then we can do so for the next and the next. Then suddenly without even realizing, at some point we'll discover that we have transfigured ourselves into a being of great light through the power of our thoughts; a being that has power over death and a love so great that through grace it melts the illusion of others.

The future is being written this moment, malleable to our intent. The past, too, loses its painful tyranny over the present as we transmute its heartache to wisdom. If neither the fear of the future nor the pain of the past any longer rule our lives, we have become a free sovereign being. No longer do we seek truth here or there, but instead create it moment by moment in mastery and in light. There is only this moment. Let us seize it with determination and pivot our lives from victimhood to skillful mastery and by some chance we may discover that all the cosmos pivots with us.

Failing Successfully

A day without failure is a day without growth. Our battle in life is not against outside circumstances. After all, one strengthens that which one opposes. The true battle of a light promoter is against illusion. Every encounter with opposition is a chance to pierce the illusion and find the hidden perception. In that case, how can we really ever fail?

To put it more clearly, the man in the street who tries to triumph without learning a thing has everything to lose and nothing to gain. If he ends up being 'right', in his mind he has triumphed. All he has really managed to do as he tries to force his belief systems onto others or circumstances, is to thicken the prison bars that keep him locked in his world view.

Because the light promoter knows that his being is his sustenance, he is unconcerned by others' opinion of him; thus he has nothing to prove and everything to learn. Because his nurturer parents and nurtures his inner child, his warrior protects his inner family and the sage guides those inner pieces, he does not ever have to live up to the expectations of others. He has ceased to need. Being self-referring for approval, he can sit back and enjoy the success of learning from his mistakes, becoming more and more filled with light.

The most common mistake made when confronted with a challenge is to measure it against past experience. This leads us to believe we have it identified and labeled. To avoid this there are four steps we use in order to avoid strengthening old belief systems and failing to grasp the insights.

1. We don't back away from a challenge if it is ours to tackle.
We remind ourselves of the covenant we made with the Infinite to find understanding through our experiences. Firstly, the challenge is ours to fight if there is still a knee–jerk reaction (which

means un-yielded insights) versus just a feeling of tedium signaling that we have already learned this lesson and don't need to play the old game again. The challenge needs to be backed away from till another day if your skill level is not up to tackling it and it could be dangerous. Secondly, the destiny we have undertaken requires many insights to successfully complete. We cannot skip pieces of the puzzle. Therefore, we embrace a challenge if it is ours.

2. **We know that there is far more to this challenge than just its initial appearance.** We take time to see behind the appearances, because we are ever mindful that what we have undertaken to solve is uniquely ours. It can not be compared to anything anyone else has ever experienced.

3. **We remind ourselves that we are really working on our destiny.** Our destiny is to solve that portion of the mystery of the Infinite's being for which we took sole responsibility. When we do this, failure versus success becomes meaningless. The only failure in the true meaning of the word is failure to learn.

4. **We realize that we created this challenge.** We did so by carefully manifesting outside circumstances to learn our next insight. We further remember that the solution has to benefit the indwelling life of all involved. If we fail to learn our lessons, others who have contracted to mirror certain things to us get trapped on the treadmill with us. Living our highest truth always benefits all.

Once again the key to successfully living these principles depends on inclusiveness; seeing the large picture. The following words by President Woodrow Wilson summarize this principle: "I would rather fail in a cause I know one day will triumph, than triumph in a cause that I know one day will fail."

The Attitude of Grace

As the surfer becomes the wave and the skier becomes the mountain, as a dancer becomes the drum, so the master becomes one with the currents and flow of the river of life. Flowing fluidly around the rocks in the river, cooperating with the whirls and eddies along the way, the master becomes a skillful epitome of ultimate grace.

The attitude of living with grace is a composite of various factors that blend into one admirable quality, inspiring to observe and imperative to cultivate, for higher consciousness awaits the one who does. But higher consciousness always goes hand in hand with increased energy; therefore grace must in some way yield more energy.

Living life with grace conserves energy, for the sensitive co-operation with life does not allow for frivolous squandering of energy through fighting battles that aren't ours or through attempting to control either outcomes or others. Energy further is conserved by mastering the element of timing, one of the factors that create a life of grace.

There is a moment to act and a moment to cease. There is a moment to advance and another to retreat. In order for us to give each moment its proper due, we have to be in a state of stillness to hear the promptings of the voice of God. We also have to be in a state of heightened awareness to watch for the indicating signs in our environment.

The other key component of grace is fluidity. The fluid being does not bring the last moment into the present. Though the last may have been a catastrophe, life spins on a dime and if we enter the next moment without expectation, the ability to salvage the day may yet present itself. The past becomes a ball and chain if we drag it into the future:

"The moving finger writes:
And having writ, Moves on: nor all thy Piety
Nor wit shall lure it back to cancel
Half a line, Nor all thy tears wash out
A word of it."
Rubaiyat of Omar Khayyam (Persian poet, 11th century)

The fluid grace we bring to our lives has no hint of rigid resistance. Grace is not ashamed to cry nor afraid to grieve, for having opened up to the torrential outpouring of life moving through us we weep when it weeps and dance when it dances. We have entered the impersonal life of mastery.

The final component of grace is excellence–that gilding of the fruits of our labor as they are offered up to the glory of God. My life is dedicated to excellence. My soul withers in the face of mediocrity. I want to think only the loftiest thoughts possible and dream only dreams of unsurpassed beauty. I want to celebrate the ordinary moments of each day and leave blessings with each footprint. I want to walk a path of grace upon the earth.

The Majesty of Poise

The calm poise detected in masters of power is the culmination of a lifetime of discipline and the unconditional surrender to the unfolding of life. It is the crowning glory of a life well lived; a life in which the larger vision was the determining factor rather than a focus on the vicissitudes of every day life.

When we observe from a mountain top the journey of a bicycle in the valley below, it may appear as a straight course, but nothing can be further from the truth. The bicycle moves slightly left then right and back again constantly. If we hold the larger vision in our lives, the daily to's and fro's appear inconsequential. Calmness replaces attempts to control the inevitable instabilities that are inherent in the journey.

If there are times when the rageful onslaught of another can easily throw off the balance we have worked so hard to achieve, then we have already conceded defeat. The eagle is the mortal enemy of the heron, but naturalists have seen attacks by an eagle on the heron in which the heron stood in perfect stillness and poise, beak pointed at the sky. The eagle in a dive of ferocious speed and focused intent, in these instances, impaled himself on the heron's beak.

Should we still be the target of another's rage, let us stand just like the heron in the majesty of calmness, never leaving the center of our circle. It may become clear that universal energy conspires to assist the one who stands in strength and poise far more readily than the one who plays the part of helpless victim.

The essence of calmness is to not anticipate or control life, but instead, to let life come to us. So too with those who are our teachers disguised as our enemies. By all means prepare for the worst, for to be taken by surprise drains energy, but having done so we have earned the right to expect the best. Under the gaze of calmness the absence of luster in the lives of our opponents becomes apparent. The only power they find they can muster is a destructive one and thus they can only peck at the object of their discomfort in an attempt to reduce him to their level.

Calmness and poise are tested by interaction and adversity, but it is fed by solitude. If solitude is the price of greatness, I would gladly pay, and should I chafe under the burden of it, I would remind myself of the alternative: a life lived in the half-light, enslaved by approval and condemned to beg for alms of well-being from another.

We study and quote the great ones of history, but instead, if we value the inspiration of the divine within, we shall join those great ones.

Self–Reliance

Great gains in self–reliance have been made during the last 25 to 30 years, in large part as the result of an escalating de-structuring of family life. For every loss there is a gain, and in this instance both men and women have been plunged into single parent units where they have had to play many roles and often find at the end of a weary day that the only nurturing afforded them will have to be self-nurturing.

Furthermore, there is no one to fight their battles and after bitter lessons they may also be fortunate enough to stumble onto the great truth that has separated genius from mediocrity; that no one can advise us on a course of action–not even the angels themselves. They can only illuminate eternal truths as guiding lights upon our way. Our paths, unique only to us, lie on an uncharted course and the compass is found in the higher wisdom whispered through the promptings of our hearts. Then suddenly one day, a starkly revealed truth emerges and we realize that our being is our sustenance.

Such a realization is indeed the very foundation of self-reliance. It is only the beginning, however, for the edifice to be built upon it takes the painstaking effort of casting off the enslavement of social conditioning and laying the bricks of original thought moment by luminous moment.

Original thought does not ask whether the world can understand it, for its origin is the heart of God and to enter there, linear and superficial thought must be left at the gate. The world wallows in conformity and society favors mediocrity over greatness. To ask for either its understanding or its approval is to sound the death knell to originality. The eagle who has seen the whole valley from the higher thermals above, attempting to mingle with the flocks of birds on the ground would find only rejection. For the pigeons know that in the presence of the eagle their own lack of sight is made all the more apparent.

Relinquishing either the need to please or the need to have others conform to our expectations creates a sovereignty and peace of mind. It would be as though, instead of walking around with an umbilical cord that we are trying to plug into another, we were to plug it back into ourselves. We would find ourselves then as our own source of strength and nurturing, self-supporting and self-referring for approval.

To such a one, life may bring what it will, for nothing can rob or erode their greatest treasure...the peace of mind inner sovereignty brings.

Reverence

Reverence stems from the ability to glimpse the divine within form and it also enhances that ability. In that moment when the heavens reveal themselves through the eyes of a child or unfurl with the dew-soft petals of a rose, a reverent response arises in our hearts. To the eyes of profanity the doors concealing the divine remain closed; whereas the more we approach life prepared to be awe-inspired, the more we shall be.

If there are parts of Creation we exclude from our reverence, let us look a little deeper and there too we can find abundant reasons for seeing the perfection of indwelling life. Some revere the beauty of the flowers in their garden, but shun the weeds. The virulence of life and the determination to survive found in the weeds is a true testimony to the universal law that we strengthen that which we oppose.

It is often easier to feel reverence for nature or the genius reflected in the works of man's hands, than for our fellow man. The reverence may not appear at all unless we learn at last to embrace the value of folly. The grandest of souls assigned the task of solving the most ambitious part of the mystery of beingness, might appear at times more foolish than the complacent person who stays in the safety of the known.

Perhaps we sanctimoniously think it is our duty as a light promoter to withhold our recognition of the value of Lucifer and his hosts of darkness. Without them there would be no material life. If they had not loved us enough to enter into the deep forgetfulness to play this role, we would have had to do so, for everything the plan of Creation was designed to accomplish hinges on the opposite pole of Creation being embodied by one third of individuated beings.

Reverence leaves the mark of refinement upon the one who makes it a way of life. Refinement is often misunderstood as belonging to one who is educated or steeped in culture, but it belongs as much to the farmer who kneels in the mud cradling the newborn lamb tenderly with work worn hands. It is the hallmark of one who recognizes the infinite value of life as the embodiment of the Divine.

I can no more spit on the ground than I can in the face of another. For while in states of expanded awareness I have seen the true glory of the earth. I have seen that the very dirt upon which we stand glows with a light more beautiful than the most breath-taking sunset. I know that every blade of grass shares my reverence for life. Scientists have measured a response that can only be described as a silent scream in plants when a fly is killed in their vicinity.

The answer to pollution, poverty and homelessness is not more technology, it is reverence for the purposes of indwelling life in order to co-operate with it. Light promoters tend to want to save and fix–this still judges and divides whereas acknowledging wholeness heals.

Generosity

If there is one thing that characterizes nature perhaps more than anything else, it is abundance. Spring does not just bring one flower, the pine tree does not produce just one seed and everywhere we look, teeming life speaks of the generous abundance within the natural world.

Generosity is the allowing of this natural abundance to use us as a vehicle. It is therefore simply life giving to itself. The person of vision will realize that to withhold is not an option. For the minute we close ourselves to the flow of life, we not only close ourselves to giving but also to receiving and stagnation and atrophy occur. To illustrate this:

Two little ponds nestled side by side on the mountain top. "I wonder what's over the edge", said one little pond. "Perhaps I ought to take a look." "Don't do it!", said the other little pond in alarm. "Save your water in case you dry up."

But the first little pond edged towards the cliff and seeing the wonderful world below, poured himself over the side of the mountain. He tumbled down as a waterfall and flowed into a small stream where cows drank and children played and where flowers grew along the banks. He went all the way to the ocean and saw whales, dolphins and boats. He evaporated into the clouds where seagulls flew and saw even more. Finally, when the clouds swept up the side of the mountain, he rained down next to the second little pond.

"Whee!", he said. "That was fun! I'm going again!" As he got ready to tumble over the edge again, he looked back and saw that a thin layer of slime had formed on his friend.

Generosity is life-affirming and inclusive. It helps others build rather than keeping them on the treadmill. To give and give again but find that instead of advancing, we have just perpetuated the status quo, does not serve the evolution of awareness. The gift must be proportionate to the need, however. We cannot give a homeless, jobless, hungry man $1 and not expect him to need again the following day. At the same time, supplying all his needs but not assisting him to remedy the lack of perception that caused his dilemma, is not really meeting his needs at all.

Can one really thrust perception onto another just because his hunger needs to be assuaged? Is there any assurance that this is not exactly the life he desires or was destined for? The answer to both questions must be "No". Generosity means giving at the level another is prepared to receive.

Generosity requires sensitivity; not only the sensitivity to gauge our fellow man's readiness (not worthiness, for everyone who lives and breathes is but a part of us) to receive, but also the sensitivity to assess the level at which he is capable of receiving.

Giving that is done to compensate for our own inadequacies (e.g.–we do not feel lovable, so we settle for feeling needed), is a barren gift devoid of spirit. Let us therefore give like nature, "For to withhold is to perish", asking neither for recognition nor gratitude or even self-satisfaction to sanction the deed, but because we are heirs to the Kingdom of Heaven and all that the Father has is ours.

> *"There are those who give little of the much*
> *which they have–and they give it for recognition and*
> *their hidden desire makes their gifts unwholesome.*

> *And there are those who have little and give it all.*
> *These are the believers in life and the bounty of life,*
> *and their coffer is never empty..."*
> *Giving*, by Kahlil Gibran (The Prophet)

Why Immortality is a Goal When Our Being is Eternal

In the 3rd and final stage of human evolution, the master changes from mortal to immortal. During the second phase of this stage, the flesh becomes incorruptible and fully spiritualized. There are few who understand the significance of this event and fewer yet who write or speak about it.

If we can understand how the reflection of the Infinite, that which is unreal (Creation), can become real when the higher bodies of the Infinite flood its material body with light and love, we can understand our own experience. The spiritualizing or making real of our body is to us, just as it is to the Infinite, the next step in the evolution of awareness.

It is also the way we can contribute most in our service to the One Life. Although we are in our highest identity not a small particle, but a unique perspective of the whole, we shall pretend we are a cell in the body of the Infinite. When a body becomes eternal or spiritualized matter, it occurs as follows:

• The light quotient–the total volume of internalized light–reaches a critical mass stage. It becomes more than a mortal body in its present stage of evolution can contain.

• Cells start to transfigure one by one into immortal matter and again this reaches a critical mass. Only so many cells can transfigure before the whole body transfigures.

• When anything transfigures to a higher level, there is a release of energy. The energy comes from that which was tied up in keeping the illusion present in the previous stage. New energy to facilitate further transfiguration of the remaining cells becomes available.

• The increased energy yields the power needed for transfiguration.

• When the being (whether it is one of us or the Infinite) becomes so light filled and, at a cellular level, so transfigured that complete transfiguration is inevitable, the pineal gland discharges a lightning flash of energy. The flash of energy through the body transfigures it entirely from mortal to immortal.

• Therefore, if we equate our physical body to a cell within the body of the Infinite, the personal transfiguration into an immortal being sets off a chain reaction throughout material life. This enables all other cells to reach the same state much more easily. In other words, we help evolve the awareness of all Creation and because any being's evolution begins with its denser parts, we also contribute to the evolution of the One.

• Our own evolution also receives a huge shot in the arm as well from the energy now available that had previously been tied up in maintaining the illusion of death.

A true warrior of light does not give up his or her power to anything, including the tyranny of death. He or she strives in every way possible to gain sovereignty and become a free being, able to come and go between realms, taking the body along. Such a one has become the master of his or her own destiny, knowing that after a life of discipline, death can no longer snuff out the flame of life.

"I was crowned by my God, my crown is living....
I received the face and the fashion of a new person...
And the thought of truth led me on.

I walked after it and did not wander.
And all that have seen me were amazed and
I was regarded by them as a strange person.
And he who knew and brought me up is the
Most High in all his perfection and He glorified me by his
kindness and raised my thoughts to the height of His truth.
And from thence He gave me the way of His precepts and
I opened the doors that were closed.
And broke in pieces the bars of iron; but my iron
melted and dissolved before me;
Nothing appeared closed to me,
because I was the door of everything."
Odes of Solomon (Apocrypha)

Opening the Chakras

Chakras are energy vortices that act as interfaces between the levels of light in the cosmos and the physical. Light is received by the chakras acting as storage units or capacitors. They then download it to the physical component designed to receive light, at a rate able to be received. The main physical components within the human body are the endocrine glands. However, each cell is also equipped with its own miniscule chakra system.

The earth too has her chakras, and the opening of the seven seals as described in the Bible (Revelations), refer specifically to the earth's opening of her chakras in preparation for her ascension. Where do these seals or plugs come from?

As trauma or forced change (pain) occurs, there is often a delay in processing the insights the experience yields. In the case of the earth we have to process it for her. The accumulation of these suppressed insights creates a blockage or plug in the center of the chakra. Most people therefore have chakras that are conical to the front and back.

As we start living self-examined lives and extract the insights from past experience, the chakras release their seals and become spherical. The more we become aware of the purpose of indwelling life hiding behind form, the more our chakras open and overlap. Eventually, there is one large unified chakra field. Heartache, sexual stimulation, expanded awareness, and other feelings usually localized within the area of a chakra, now are felt in the entire body.

When the chakra fields unify, a lot more energy is available to the individual and inner guidance becomes strong. The reason for this is that obstruction from the mental body is partially reduced and the influence of the higher bodies floods into the lower bodies. One begins to live in grace; to cooperate with the higher self in living the blueprint for this particular life.

Just prior to entry into God-consciousness, a most miraculous experience transfigures the chakra field yet again. The symbol for this event was depicted by the ancients as a dove, beak pointed upwards wings extended in a sphere or circle. This signifies the opening of five additional chakras utilized by someone in the second (God-consciousness) and third (Immortal Master) stage.

The additional five chakras open as a result of incorporating all seven supporting attitudes into our lives. Their opening happens in a matter of minutes, unlike the more gradual opening of the other seven. This event may be preceded by physical discomfort and some bruising that comes and goes over major acupuncture points like the wrists.

The experience itself however is blissful and expansive. White light surrounds the body and a violet flame is visible on the head (like the description in the Bible of the flames during Pentecost, visible on the heads of those present). The light has a particular configuration resembling a dove with a circle above its head.

The opening occurs as follows:

1. The areas of the body where a woman's ovaries would be located burst open with white light, first the left, and then immediately the right as chakras eight and nine open;
2. A skirt of light radiates downward, resembling the tail of the dove;
3. This ignites the pranic tube and a great rush of energy travels up from the base of the spine to the crown of the head and the violet flame appears;
4. Immediately afterwards a sphere of light about the size of a dinner plate appears about 8" above the head. It looks like the Sumerian and Egyptian art, depicting the spheres above the heads of those of spiritual power. The tenth chakra is now open;
5. The eleventh chakra in the middle of the right shoulder blade and the twelfth chakra in the middle of the left shoulder blade next open and shoot out wings of light. Angelic beings, who have all twelve chakras open have been portrayed as having wings by those who can see energy directly;
6. The entire configuration of light at this point appears like a dove with a sphere above its head. There is a hidden reason however, why the ancients had the dove enclosed by the circle, rather than having it above the head. The secret lies in the name the Lemurians gave to the number 10 (remember, the circle or sphere above the head is the tenth chakra). The number ten is called "lahun" in Lemurian and some other ancient languages. "La" means all and "hun" means one (la is "all" backwards and languages still have words like "un" or "uno" etc. for one);

The number ten means all in one and one in all (the Atlanteans also knew these secrets behind the law of the one). The sphere above the head will become larger and larger as we progress into the later stages of God-consciousness. At first it will extend all the way to the head, cleaving the flame into two 'horns' on either side (also depicted in ancient art). Eventually, when the Immortal Master overcomes all mortal boundaries, the sphere will enclose all other chakras–all is in one and one is in all.

Such a master now has the vehicle to travel at will with the speed of thought between dimensions and through space and time. The dove is now in the circle. The epitome of what a human being can be has been achieved.

The Human DNA Template

The human DNA is the road map to the cosmos. It is a road map of such detailed frequency that it can be used to create language and an ancient form of writing that precedes letters–sigels. Many mystery schools and enlightened cultures patterned themselves in one way or another after the DNA template because of the power it has in representing the macro-cosmos.

When viewed in cross section by someone able to see frequency, the DNA strand would resemble the rose. (See Figure 15, DNA Frequency Chambers) In looking at the rose pattern, we are looking at the frequency patterns that occur throughout the cosmos; governmental structure of Mu and a map of the 4th dimensional city in the Himalayas, Shambala. It is also found in the Christian cathedral rose windows. The rose pattern represents the orders of ancient female (goddess) mystery schools that once existed on earth. Sadly, most were prematurely exterminated, taking the secrets of the DNA activation through frequency with them until now.

The power held in the pattern of the frequency template that exists throughout Creation can be used in establishing government,

DNA Frequency Chambers

Goddess Archetypes

Seven Lords of Light

Arakana (Arachne)

Yod Hay Vau

(Figure 15)

in drawing the sigel of your name, or in developing a map of evolution. For instance, throughout many lifetimes initiates would move from one through thirteen of the mystery schools in order to master the thirteen facets of the divine feminine and the accompanying attitudes that would activate the frequency chambers of the DNA.

During the thirteen lunar cycles of each year (from new moon to new moon) we can live the principles embodied by each of the goddess orders, focusing particularly on the specific one of that moon cycle. We end the year by exploring Ara-ka-na, practicing on allowing the aggression and negativity of others to move through us as we become a portal.

The power of a sigel for one's name lies in the energy behind the spoken word. (See Figure 16, Using the Frequency Template to Create Sigels) If we take the name Michael for instance, it maps out the individual's contract with the Infinite; their destiny and the frequency that is their unique perspective within the universe. An advanced being knows that the frequency of the name contains its essence, or meaning. He will know that 'Mi' is consciousness, 'Ka' is energy and 'El' is matter, revealing that the entity so named has undertaken to step consciousness through energy down to matter. El also means 'lord', and Mi-ka-el is also lord of consciousness and energy.

The petals in the rose pattern of DNA are various sound chambers of frequency activated by attitude. Someone who follows the right-brain method of ascension would use praise, love, and gratitude, activating the three middle petals or sound chambers. These three main attitudes activate the seven supporting attitudes (and vice versa): grace, reverence, self-reliance, calmness and poise, the embracing of failure as a learning tool, the ability to work with time and live in the moment, and generosity. These attitudes bring the middle row of seven sound chambers on line. Incorporating the

Using the Frequency Template to Create Sigels

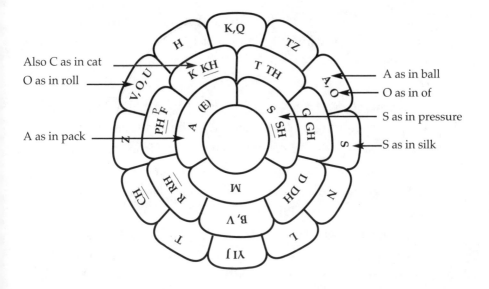

Also C as in cat

O as in roll

A as in pack

A as in ball

O as in of

S as in pressure

S as in silk

The sigel on the template spells out Michael (Mi-ka-el)

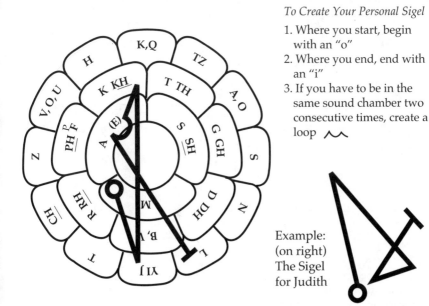

To Create Your Personal Sigel

1. Where you start, begin with an "o"
2. Where you end, end with an "i"
3. If you have to be in the same sound chamber two consecutive times, create a loop ⋀⋀

Example: (on right) The Sigel for Judith

(Figure 16)

thirteen divine feminine attitudes activates the twelve outer petals, and the doorway within the center of the DNA opens. The person becomes a positively charged being within a negatively charged Creation.[7]

The sound or frequency chambers activate the corresponding DNA strands, bringing them 'on line'. Thus attitude can be used to activate the strands, 10 of which are formed from sub-atomic particles. In a left-brained person the strands are activated through insights gained and that in turn activates the sound chambers or corresponding petals of the rose.

In the same way that our names emphasize our unique mission or destiny in the cosmos, our DNA chambers are emphasized in a specific and unique pattern as well. This provides us with a unique perspective and placement of the assemblage point that in turn gives us a unique way of looking at the world (one could say it gives our world a special flavor).

This is done because material life is like the eyes and hands (the physical body) of the Infinite. Diversity at this level of density is essential, especially diversity of perception. Note also that material life is in the South[8] and we previously mentioned that the tool of dreaming in the South utilizes the change in the placement of the assemblage point for accessing non-cognitive information. In this way we all have unique perspectives.

---

7 For more detailed information, readers are referred to the book *A Life of Miracles* and to audio recordings *Flowers of the Heart* and *Journey to the Heart of God, IV*.

8 See discussion in section titled *The True Nature of The Seven Directions* in Chapter 1.

CHAPTER THREE

THE MYSTERIES OF THE ARCHETYPES

Archetypes As Part Of The Cosmos

The fields of the human brain resemble a dodecahedronal field around each of its hemispheres. A dodecahedron looks like a soccer ball with twelve pentagons connected at each of their five sides, creating a faceted sphere. The left brain has a dodecahedron with twelve pentagons, but the right brain has a dodecahedron with twelve pentagons and an additional pentagon in the middle.

These facets represent aspects of the divine masculine and the divine feminine; the god archetypes and the goddess archetypes. Part of our evolution of awareness is to incorporate these aspects into our lives and merge the left brain's field with the right brain's field.

An example of how a left brain aspect (represented by a pentagon) merges with a right brain one, would be as follows:

If someone were to have mastered the ability to manifest money whenever needed, he wouldn't concern himself with expenditures or having to save or to buy insurance. Whenever there is a bill, he somehow finds the money to pay for it. One day, however, he notices he is suddenly starting to run into debt; the funds aren't manifesting as they used to.

He has already learned how to create a flow of supply (the goddess aspect). It has become time to master the god, or left brain facet of supply, which is the ability to harness and plan, budget and regulate by projecting what income will be necessary to meet demands. This new set of skills, in conjunction with the right brain skills, will enable him to master harnessing the flow of supply throughout other areas of his life, such as time management.

When these two specific aspects are fully integrated into his life, the two pentagon facets of the fields around the brain halves meld into one, like a sacred marriage of the divine masculine and feminine. When all twelve pairs have "married" as aspects of our lives, the sacred fire (kundalini) rises through the pranic tube and the chakras burst open.

What is applicable to man is also applicable to the planet and, ultimately, the Infinite and its Creation as well. Since 1998 the fields around the planet have been merging their facets and within the next years the opening of her seven chakras will take place.

This process precedes entry into God-consciousness and involves thirteen goddess facets plus twelve god facets and seven neutral elements (chakras), equaling thirty-two total components. To represent these aspects, thirty-two gods, goddesses and neutral archangels abide to oversee Creation; we shall call them the creator gods, although they are the 5th tier or level down from One, the Goddess of all Creation.

Because of the vast importance the earth and man are playing within the big scheme, aspects of these thirty-two creator gods have come to earth and created bodies for themselves that resemble man. They created very large caverns within the crust of the earth, including the Halls of Amenti,

"...that they might dwell eternally there, living with life to eternity's end. Thirty and two were there of the children, Sons of Light, who had come among men seeking to free from the bondage of darkness those who were bound by the force from beyond."
The Emerald Tablets of Thoth, Tablet II

They represent and oversee thirty-two aspects of life on earth and also thirty-two geographical areas; twenty (thirteen goddesses and seven neutral chakras) are on the surface of the earth, and twelve god aspects represented by geographical areas are within the earth. .

Also upon thrones of light in Amenti, but not in the form of man, are seven Lords of Light that dwelled on earth in a previous cycle of life. Only seven are mentioned in the Emerald Tablets as the additional two were called to service only as we entered the 4th dimension in March 2005. (See Figure 17, The Seven Lords of Light) The additional two lords will be discussed in the next book. Together with the great master, the Dweller also known as Horlet, they direct the destiny of humankind.

The god and goddess archetypes are represented by pentagons (five sided figures). Each side touches a side of another pentagon; therefore each pentagon interacts with five others.

For example, one of the sides of the pentagon representing the god, Lord Ki-as-mus, would be touching that of Lord Karama since they work together to balance the way the cosmos unfolds. Lord Ki-as-mus designs the time and space in which this outbreath

The Seven Lords of Light

LORD 3   Untanas
Lord of the Halls of the Dead. He is the director of negativity that is allowed to enter the earth's plane.

LORD 4   Quertas
Lord of Life. He is the giver of lifeforce who frees the souls of humankind.

LORD 5   Chietal
Lord of the power of intent. He is the giver of the frequency that forms life.

LORD 6   Goyana
Lord of hidden mysteries. He is the guardian of powers bestowed upon men, protecting the path of light from those unworthy.

LORD 7   Huertal
Lord of space and time. He works with the purpose of life and the process by which the purpose unfolds.

LORD 8   Semveta
Lord of karma and cycles for humankind. He weighs the hearts of man.

LORD 9   Ardal
Lord of white light. He turns chaos into order.

Horlet
Governs all life on earth and guards the stability of the planetary axis. Also known as the Dweller.

(Figure 17)

of God will unfold. Lord Karama decides when and where during this Creational cycle, the unresolved portions of life need to be experienced in order to solve them.

The gods work with measure (the matrix) and the timing in which Creation will unfold. The goddesses, on the other hand, work with how it unfolds (movement) and fill in the creative details, overseeing the quality of the journey.

Archetypes Within Daily Life

Our failure to comprehend the necessity for individuals to balance the archetypes within has created distortions in the way these archetypes are expressed in everyday life. Some examples are:

• In many cultures where spiritual practices and enduring spiritual traditions are a way of life, men have autonomy over these areas of life. Examples include the Jewish, Tibetan and indigenous cultures. Because women are barred from fully participating in the spiritual practices of these cultures, they have attracted suppression from races that are more masculine.

• The movement of women into the job market, corporate world and factories–the domain of the male–has often come at a cost. They have had to hide their goddess tendencies in order to compete and 'fit in'. In other words, women have had to forfeit their essence, becoming more like men to be acceptable in these environments.

• In most cultures men find it 'embarrassing' to be in anyway engaged in the goddess aspects of life, especially in front of other men who might suspect them of homosexuality. They therefore live barren and stark lives and because the overbalancing of maleness causes separateness, they live disconnectedly from the web of life. This causes great damage to the environment, great disregard for the coming generation and disrespect for the sacred traditions of others.

• In medieval Europe the sacred rites were performed by women and acknowledged to be the domain of the goddess. After the extermination of between 9-10 million women (10% are estimated to have been children), these rites were performed only by men and turned into a ridiculous parody of their original holy nature. The Inquisition had successfully suppressed the expression of the divine feminine.

When men are taught the goddess traditions, they often have responses such as the following: "Well, you placed great emphasis on this information, so it must be important, but how is it relevant to me? …Oh, by the way, can the class have a dinner for you at the end of our week together to celebrate what we've learned?"

When I then point out that he has just demonstrated two goddess aspects, those of Alu-mi-na (Goddess of celebration) and of Hay-hu-ka (Goddess who tricks into learning), he's amazed.

The dynamic balance that familiarizing ourselves with these archetypes and living them brings, prepares us for God-consciousness. Studying a goddess aspect for every one of the thirteen moon cycles of the year and a god archetype for every month is usually a very successful approach.

The archetypes should preferably be studied in the order given since they build on one another. Many students are concerned whether their chakras are 'open', failing to understand that until this sacred marriage of masculine and feminine takes place, the child (the rising of the kundalini to open the chakras) cannot be born.

The Seven Lords Of Light

"Far from the future, formless, yet forming, came
they as teachers for the children of men …

*Masters are they of the Great Secret Wisdom, brought
from the future of infinity's end."*
Emerald Tablets, Tablet III

From cycles beyond us the Seven Lords of Light have come to govern various aspects of the powers that sustain life on earth. These seven lords (Lords 3 through 9, since Lords 1 and 2 are lords of chaos and darkness) once walked the earth during its previous cycles of life long before the advent of man. (See Figure 17, The Seven Lords of Light) Governing all life on earth is the Dweller, the great Light that gives life to the earth. The Lord of the Lords of Seven, however, is the ninth lord, Ardal, who regulates the evolution of humankind. The Dweller has never incarnated on earth during any life cycle; his influence comes from many cycles beyond us to fulfill this great and luminous task.

Within the Halls of Amenti the Flower of Life, also called the cold fire and life-force center of the earth, grew. The thirty-two thrones of the Children of Light are placed around it and they use its radiance to perpetually renew their bodies. These immortal sons and daughters of Light have incarnated many times among humankind to teach and guide its evolution. They represent facets of awareness of life on earth and by their presence, strengthen these facets, maintaining order and preventing the earth from being subject to chaos.

Before we can comprehend what is represented by the Seven Lords of Light, the Dweller and the thirty-two guides of great light, we need to consider the following:

To understand the earth we need to understand ourselves.[9] The left brain of man has twelve facets representative of the twelve god archetypes. This refers to the field or sacred geometry of the

9 Suggested listening is our CD *Internal Technology 1.*

137

left brain. The right brain has thirteen facets, representing the thirteen facets of the goddess.

The seven chakras receive and interpret the seven levels of light in existence within the cosmos by receiving these levels of light from the seven bodies. The seven bodies of man are all formed from and are transmitters of these seven light frequencies. Thus the first to receive the seventh ray (violet) is the spirit body, which also receives all seven rays and is therefore the body of white light. It is then passed on to the crown chakra which downloads this violet light in the form of subtle information to its corresponding part of the endocrine system, the pineal.

Because the earth is the habitat of man, she has the same components. She is therefore as special and unique among planets as humans are among species. As among humankind, the diversity found in the life that flourishes upon her is unheard of anywhere else.

The Seven Lords of Light represent the seven levels of light that permeate the cosmos and are received by the earth's chakras. They therefore also represent the earth's seven bodies discussed in Chapter 1, The True Nature of the Seven Directions.

The Dweller can be said to represent the pranic tube that in man runs from the crown straight through to the perineum and is paralleled in the energetic structure of the earth, running through its center to bring life force and stability to the planet. If the Dweller were to withdraw his support we would immediately have an axis tilt.

The thirty-two planetary light-bearers, the Children of the Light from higher spheres, represent the following:

• Twelve represent the god archetypes;
• Thirteen represent the goddess archetypes;
• Seven represent the seven levels of light or the seven chakras and bodies of the earth, just as the Seven Lords of Light do.

138

The Sacred Symbols

In understanding the thirty-two sacred symbols representing these facets, please be aware of the following:

• The symbols stand for an actual light-filled being in the Halls of Amenti as well as an actual archetypical principle in the case of the gods and goddesses;

• The source of the earth's life force is housed in a great temple of light in the Halls of Amenti and is protected by the Halls of the Dead from unwanted intruders.

The symbols, thirty-two in all plus one for the Dweller, are keys to vast bodies of knowledge. (See Figure 18, The Twenty Sacred Symbols) For instance, there are thirty-two different realities available to man that can be assembled by moving and maintaining the position of the assemblage point. It will be found that this ancient hidden knowledge has echoes in many spiritual paths. Some temples have sixteen masculine and sixteen feminine pillars just like the sixteen upper and sixteen lower teeth guard the temple of the human skull.

There are physical, geographical areas that gather the different levels of concentrated light from these great beings that act as conductors. They too are represented by these symbols. There are twenty on the surface of the planet and twelve within. The earth's surface can be divided into an icosahedron, a Platonic solid that has twenty facets, all having identical characteristics. The icosahedronal energy field around the earth can be seen in weather patterns for example, and has been confirmed by scientists like Bruce Cathie and Buckminster Fuller.

The Twenty Sacred Symbols

The icosahedronal field around the earth and the placement
of the 20 sacred symbols: the 13 goddess symbols and the 7 symbols
of the Lords of Light. The 12 god symbols are within the earth in a
dodecahedronal pattern.

Many temples were built on sites where the energy represented
by the symbol was felt at its most intense concentration.

(Figure 18)

The Lords and Their Symbols

"Meditate on the symbols I give thee, keys are they,
though hidden of men."
Emerald Tablets, Tablet III

1. **Untanas**–The Keeper of the Halls of the Dead. He quenches life and the right to incarnate when light or the life-force is greatly diminished through resistance to life. In this way he plays his part in the evolution of awareness. The soul or life-force of man appears as floating flames of various degrees of brightness in the Halls of the Dead. When the light grows to a great luminosity, he sets that individual free from the bondage of death. He is called Lord Three.

2. **Quertas**–The one who gives life to form. As Untanas quenches life by 'swallowing' the flame with his darkness, so Quertas kindles the flame of indwelling life, called the inner fire, to bring life to form. He is the one that will gauge when humanity's light has grown bright enough to be set free from mortality. He is Lord Four.

3. **Chietal**–Holds the key to the power of intent. He is the great lord of manifestation who guards and guides the abilities of humankind to manipulate reality. Humans are endowed with abilities to manifest reality that astonish higher races. This entire holographic environment of denser material life is held in place by our minds. We daily manifest our environment but because our thoughts have tended to be chaotic, we have manifested a large degree of chaos, not realizing how powerful we are. This is monitored in a way that allows the race to fulfill its destiny and not prematurely self-destruct. Chietal is Lord Five.

4. **Goyana**–Is responsible for the initiations and the unveiling of

the mysteries along a path of enlightenment. The sacred powers and keys must be guarded from the eyes of the profane, yet accessed by those who have relinquished their personal desires upon the altar of enlightenment. Many keys to knowledge are hidden in language and symbols. He is Lord Six.

5. **Huertal**–Master of space and time, he regulates the earth's various timelines and the speed at which time passes. For example, we are coming to a close of many cycles and in preparation many karmic requirements must be met. Time feels as though it has sped up–two years feels like ten. But time is actually slowed down in order to fit everything into the few years remaining in the old cycles. In other words, time is compressed (as in the moments before an accident when it seems like an eternity) so we can fit more into it. Every two years may have ten years of change and hardships and growth packed into them. Huertal opens up the ability to travel through time and space to those who have mastered themselves. He is Lord Seven.

6. **Semveta**–He is the weigher of human hearts and works with timing. The great service density brings is that rapid growth is possible because of it and it acts as a timing mechanism. Density can either be used by the aware lightseeker to speed up progress by transmuting hardship to wisdom, or it will slow the progress of others who choose to stay on the treadmill of karma longer by failing to learn their lessons. Timing is vitally important in any evolution or else the growth will lack strength. An example is the struggle of the chicken emerging from an egg–if we pull the chicken out sooner than it would have emerged on its own, it lacks the strength to survive. Semveta is Lord Eight.

7. **Ardal**–is the Lord of the Seven, holder of white light and the keeper of keys. The master orchestrating chaos and order, he works with humanity's destiny. He balances the unfolding of

the purpose of the Infinite through individuals as well as the race into which they incarnate. He keeps chaos at bay.

> *"Few there were among the children of man who*
> *looked upon that mighty face and lived, for not as*
> *the sons of men, are the Children of Light when*
> *they are not incarnate in a physical body."*
>
> *Emerald Tablets, Tablet I*

The Dweller–is the one who is in charge of the loop of time in which humankind finds itself. He is instrumental in guiding the role of humanity as a blueprint for the cosmos; the microcosms that can communicate with the I AM, the way-showers of tomorrow. He ensures that we stay on track in our pivotal role within the big picture.

The Goddess Archetypes

(See Figure 19, 13 Goddess Archetypes)

1. **Pana-Tura**–In the original mother tongue of the earth, 'Pana' means earth element or matter and 'tura' means door. Pana-tura holds the door to materialized life and from this the legend of Pandora's box was derived. The frequency emitted in materialized life calls forth that which manifests. If Pandora's box lets in disease and poisonous spiders, it's because our frequency (emotion) is distorted and poisonous.

   Pana-tura's symbol resembles a seed emerging from the earth and also the female genitals. She germinates material life (the feminine essence is germination; the masculine inseminates) and births it into form. To materialize from the ether (a tomato, for instance), life goes through the following steps: (See Figure 20, How Matter is Formed)

   • The Trinity of Indwelling Life is separated from the Trinity of

13 Goddess Archetypes

1. PANA-TURA Goddess of germination: the Mother. She is the essence of life-giving energy that births into form. She midwifes potentialities into materialization.

2. AMA-TERRA-SU Goddess of history. On earth she is the keeper of the history stored in the rocks, sand, and soil. She keeps the record of the loop of time, which is our biggest history.

3. KA-LI-MA Goddess of equity and destroyer of illusion. She brings balance by creating potentialities that can compensate for distortions that create karma.

4. ORI-KA-LA Goddess of prophecy with the farseeing eye. She is the oracle and holder of the key to changing the future.

5. AU-BA-RI Goddess of sound or frequency. She utilizes the rage of Lucifer to break up stagnant portions of Creation. She is the cosmic sound healer who works with the potential manifestation the spoken word creates.

6. HAY-HU-KA Goddess of reversal energy. She works with indwelling life's purpose to evolve awareness, through manipulating the outer currents. She is the teacher who tricks others into learning.

7. ISHANA-MA Goddess of beauty, grace and elegance. She facilitates the peaceful interaction among her children for harmonious co-habitation. She is a mediator and promotes joyful cooperation. She is the goddess of self love.

8. APARA-TURA Goddess of cycles. She is the operator who opens doors for cycles that are opening and closes doors for cycles that are closing. She celebrates the beginning and end of cycles.

9. HAY-LEEM-A Goddess of resources. She is the weigher of the consequences of today's actions on all life, including nature and future generations.

10. UR-U-AMA Goddess of creativity and inspiration. She knows true art inspires altered perception and that life should be lived creatively.

11. AMARAKU Goddess of new beginnings and forging new ways. When the old is gone, she invents a new approach. She is the innovator.

12. ALU-MI-NA Goddess who guards the unknowable. She guards the source of all spiritual knowledge from being accessed by those with impure motives. She is the gatekeeper who determines who may cross.

13. ARA-KA-NA Goddess of the power to transcend all boundaries. She is the guardian of the portal or passageway between Creator and Creation. She represents the gateway hidden within the core of human DNA that enables us to become the I AM that I AM.

(Figure 19)

How Matter is Formed

	The Matrix (a pattern of light)	The Frequency (the specific tone)	The Blueprint

STEP 1
Within the Trinity of
Indwelling Life the
blueprint is formed

*Membrane dividing
blueprint from
manifested life*

STEP 2
A corresponding fre-
quency within the
Trinity of Materializa-
tion calls the blueprint
forth. (With frequency,
like attracts like.)

(a) The blueprint starts to
push against
the membrane

*Pocket of frequency
created by devas*

(b) The blueprint is
now in the Trinity
of Materialization

*The blueprint begins
to fill the space of
like frequency*

STEP 3
The blueprint is nega-
tively charged (having
come from the Trinity
of Indwelling Life) and
attracts atoms
(positively charged–
within matter,
opposites attract.)

(a) Atoms rush into the
designated space and
arrange themselves
according to the
matrix and frequency

(b) The form is
materialized

(Figure 20)

145

Materialization by a 'membrane', called the veil in many scriptures. Though both trinities are negative in relation to the Infinite, the Trinity of Materialization is <u>positive</u> in relation to the Trinity of Indwelling Life.

• The blueprint for the tomato is held within the Trinity of Indwelling Life. The blueprint is the product of the interaction of the masculine (the matrix) with the feminine (the frequency). Imagine two circles overlapping to form a vesica pisces–the mother circle and the father circle forming the blueprint.

• The blueprint can also be called a pocket of potentiality of matter waiting to become. As yet the pocket of potentiality has not birthed through the membrane to take form.

• In order to understand the next sequence of steps, it is important to know that within Creation opposites attract if we are referring to energy and matter (atoms), but with frequency and light, the same poles attract.

• The deva responsible for working with the tomato plant decides that it is time for the tomato to be created. First, he defines the space in which the tomato will form by creating a tomato's frequency (each creation has a signature frequency) only in that space. The frequency (mother) aspect of the blueprint (pocket of potentiality) is attracted by the similar frequency played by the deva and the blueprint is pulled through the membrane.

• The pocket of potentiality, having come from the Trinity of Indwelling Life, is negatively charged–the opposite polarity to material life. With atoms and energy, opposites attract and so they rush into the pocket of potentiality to form themselves according to the blueprint of the tomato. The same principles are used by us to manifest our life's circumstances through thought and feeling. This goddess aspect births all potentials into form as we call forth our reality by emitting certain frequencies.

2. **Ama-Terra-Su**–although a cosmic goddess like all other goddess archetypes, is called by the name given to her by the ancient races on earth. 'Ama' (mother) 'terra' (earth) 'su' (awareness) is the keeper of the earth's history. Her symbol resembles a tongue, for the feminine method of history-keeping is the oral tradition. The symbol also stands for the largest history humankind has, the loop in time.

   The feminine way of storing history through the oral tradition was preferred by many cultures. They avoided the use of writing because it thrusts a civilization into being left-brain dominated. The written history tends to focus on deeds and actions while the oral history brings the emotions of the drama to life. The former focuses on the mirrors, the latter on indwelling life.

   But as we shall see in the realm of the fifth goddess, Au-ba-ri, when someone talks and others listen, thoughtforms are developed, pulling that which is spoken about into the present (in frequency and light, present in visualization, like attracts like). If tales of great heroism are told, the tribe will once again produce great heroes. If the whole tribe feels avoidance for cowardice, they will tend to avoid being cowardly. In this way history comes alive.

   If we compare the scenario described to most modern industrialized civilizations, we find that our own histories don't play a very active part in our lives. They shape the future only in a minor way and as a result, do not influence the conduct of societies like they could. How are we to learn from the past when the average person knows so little about it?

3. **Ka-Li-Ma**–There is an on-going balancing to create equity beneath the surface of life. Called by Emerson the Law of Compensation, this constant adding and subtracting to bring about justice is the domain of the goddess Ka-li-ma (ka=energy,

li=to illuminate, ma=mother); the mother of illuminating energy.

Her symbol stands for pockets of balancing potentials hanging on the membrane that separates manifested from unmanifested life. In other words, if one choice becomes reality, a balancing potential also has to manifest. The symbol also represents a scale. This goddess is often called Justina and always depicted with a scale.

For all material gain there is a price to pay. Emerson, in his Essay on The Law of Compensation, explains:

"For example, in the animal kingdom the physiologist has observed that no creatures are favored, but a certain compensation balances every gift and every defect.
A surplusage given to one part is paid out of a reduction from another part of the same creature. The theory of mechanic forces is another example: What is gained in power is lost in time; and the converse.

The same dualism underlies the nature and condition of man. Every excess causes a defect; every defect an excess."

It is an illusion that anything can be taken away from us; anything taken must be restored in some other way. The same applies to material gain. For every gain there is a loss. Injustice is an illusion and Ka-li-ma dispels illusion by bringing justice.

The justice of the goddess has to do with morality rather than the lower masculine law that deals with ethics. Morality embodies the spirit of the law and serves indwelling life. Ethics deal with the letter of the law and serve form or appearances.

That which is gained but is really part of our true nature, such as wisdom, carries no on-going penalty. It comes from the unifying field of indwelling life rather than the separatism of material life. We pay by piercing the illusion hidden within the opposition of our lives, but once the toll has been paid and the gateway to wisdom opens, it is ours to receive freely.

> *"There is no penalty to virtue, no penalty to wisdom;*
> *are proper additions of being. In a virtuous action,*
> *I properly am, in a virtuous act, I add to the world ...*
> *There can be no excess to love, none to knowledge,*
> *none to beauty, when these attributes are considered*
> *in the purest sense.*
>
> *Essay on the Law of Compensation* by Ralph Waldo Emerson

4. **Ori-Ka-La**–'Ori' (lights the way or lamp), 'ka' (energy), 'la'(all), means she who lights the way for the energy of all. She is the oracle and the visionary. She guides and holds the key to the future. The word 'key' comes from ka-la and is more noticeable in some languages (such as French) than others.

   The symbol for Ori-ka-la not only reflects the probable future held in the vesica pisces, but also the third or all-seeing eye. The reason the vesica pisces or blueprint of potential events (created by the overlapping circles of the matrix and frequency) is relevant to this goddess, is because that is where the future is kept.

   All probabilities are held within the Trinity of Indwelling Life. She sees what probable futures are most likely to be pulled through the membrane into manifestation, based on the frequencies most dominant today.

   The benefit of knowing the most probable future is that we can then change it to a more beneficial one by changing the frequency (emotion) we emit today. This is why she holds the key to everyone's future.

5. **Au-Ba-Ri**–'Au' means to listen, 'ba' is body–or sometimes baby, 'ri' is to shine or be luminous. Au-ba-ri means she who

through listening creates a luminous body. It is the origin of the name Audrey and the root for the word embryo. Her symbol represents a left ear which is governed by the right brain and implies listening with the heart. It also resembles an embryo.

The embryo as a symbol for listening is based on a principle that the oral traditions, mentioned under Ama-terra-su, rely on. When someone listens from the heart to someone speaking with emotion, a thoughtform is created between them that sets in motion the frequency that will pull in the potential. In this way their words come alive and take form. The ear is like the receptive womb, the words inseminate it and a "ba" or 'baby's embryo' is created (a potential future). Other great services rendered through listening are:

- On our journey to fulfill our destiny, we cannot find the meaning of many of our challenges from our vantage point. At times the seemingly overwhelming opposition can leave us feeling frustrated and wanting a place to vent. This type of listening doesn't require a reply or advice. It just allows the other person to relieve some of the mounting pressure.
- When we listen to another's folly, we can learn their lessons for them. Since the only reason for experience is to solve certain mysteries of beingness, our gaining the insights on their behalf can help them step off the treadmill of experiences they may have been locked onto.

6. **Hay-Hu-Ka**–'Hay' means goddess, 'hu' means indwelling life,'ka' means energy. Hay-hu-ka is the goddess of the energy of indwelling life. Her symbol represents an undercurrent since her influence is under the surface of material life. She tricks into learning and is often called the trickster or Loki, or the coyote teacher.

She uses laughter as a teaching tool and is also known as the sacred clown. She uses the ridiculous and unexpected to break up stagnant energy and to keep us from becoming pompous and taking ourselves too seriously.

She manipulates events to enable us to turn learning into experiential knowledge. She jars our perception when it becomes too narrow by giving us the reverse outcome of what was expected. She is the custodian of the powerful force of reversal energy.

Reversal energy is based on the concept of the pivot point–the fact that the largest lever still has only a single point on which the movement balances. Many cannot understand why earth, an insignificant little speck in the vastness of space, can be of such importance. The reason is that the future of the universe pivots here.

No matter how powerful the movement is in one direction, with knowledge about the pivot point, the same force can be reversed, much like the slightest tap to a spinning top can throw its rotation off. Hay-Hu-Ka uses this knowledge to reverse the currents of existence when they deviate too far off course from the purpose of indwelling life.

7. **Ishana-Ma**–'Ish' means come, 'ana' means from Heaven and 'ma' means mother. Ishana-ma is the mother who comes from heaven. As the name implies, she is concerned with creating a family life that is like heaven on earth. She is the Aphrodite archetype.

In reality the family is like a microcosm of the macrocosm. It embodies the characteristics of the races within Creation–the family of God's creatures. The smooth and harmonious interaction between these facets of the One expressing as the many is the domain and responsibility of this goddess. The future hinges on her executing these functions properly. The balance between all creatures must be established as the journey back to the heart of God begins.

She is also concerned that within the relating of one part of Creation with another, the masculine and feminine are in perfect balance. When one dominates the other, the flow of the evolution of awareness is disrupted. Her symbol is a masculine (counter-clockwise) and feminine (clockwise) spiral in perfect balance. It also shows a reflection of the Infinite to its Creation.

This goddess fosters self-regard and self-respect, the starting point for respect for others. Ishana-ma promotes the appreciation of the miracle of self; the divinity within each cell, the perfection in how form responds to individual intent. As we gratefully acknowledge the surge of lifeforce through our bodies, it increases one hundredfold.

> *"I am the poet of the body and the poet of the soul.*
> *I celebrate myself and sing myself,*
> *And what I assume, you shall assume.*
> *For every atom belonging to me as good belongs to you.*
> *I believe in the flesh and the appetites,*
> *Seeing, hearing, feeling, are miracles,*
> *and each part and tag of me is a miracle.*
> *Divine Am I inside and out, and I make holy*
> *whatever I touch or am touch'd from …*
> *If I worship one thing more than another it shall be*
> *the spread of my own body, or any part of it,*
> *Translucent mold of me it shall be you!"*
> Excerpts from Song of Myself, Walt Whitman (1819-1892)

8. **Apara-Tura**–'Apara' means operator and 'tura' means door. The word aperture comes from her name. The name Dorothea that has survived in some of our languages means the door god-

dess. Apara-tura is the operator of "doors" who opens and closes the cycles of life. Her symbol is comprised of two ancient ones:

- The brackets are found as the symbol on the ancient Norse rune that stands for opening; also used by the Druids and other ancient European cultures;
- The counterclockwise spiral can be found on the petroglyphs of many North American Tribes. It represents the closing of a cycle.

Her symbol therefore means the opening and closing of cycles. She is the goddess of birth and death and provides a perfect example of how the gods and goddesses work together. Her counterpart Ka-pa-el, determines when the energy contained within an individual, nation or race, has reached a critical high or low point that necessitates change. It is then that the goddess creates the ideal conditions for birth into a higher state of being (transfiguration) or the recycling of the atomic elements of the form (death).

She is the singer of the death song. She creates the frequency that will call the soul into the spirit world in the following ways:

- The body loses energy when it has fruitless experiences that do not give insight;
- The body's frequency becomes lowered and can no longer house the higher frequency of the soul with ease. Illness (dis-ease) occurs;
- The body's frequency eventually becomes so inhospitable that the beings functioning under the order of the god Ka-pa-el determine that a more harmonious place must be found for the soul to dwell (the soul cries out for this);
- The goddess Apara-tura creates a strong corresponding frequency within the spirit world to attract the soul out of the body; the true meaning of the concept of the death song;

• The soul leaves, cracking the luminous cocoon which then folds upon itself, resembling an embryo. Lifeforce spills out and the body dies. Trauma, such as a mortal accident, can crack the cocoon and then the soul leaves, reversing the order.

In celebrating the cycles of existence and rites of passage, Apara-tura creates history. Ama-terra-su records and tells history, but by creating the high points and low points along the journey of life, Apara-tura helps to create it. The reason the family of man does not feel united is that their common history has been forgotten. There is only national history to draw from which creates nationalism and fragments the unity of man. This goddess contributes to our sense of belonging by providing common experiences and history.

9. **Hay-Leem-A**–'Hay' means goddess, 'leem' means water and flow, 'a' means of. From this goddess the name Halima, common in the Middle East is derived. Hay-leem-a has stewardship over the supply and demand of resources. As the goddess of flow, she sees that today's actions do not deprive future generations of the supply needed to fulfill their destiny.

Within the cosmos not a thought or an action can take place without affecting the entire cosmos. Wherever a pebble falls, the ripples go on forever. Hay-leem-a oversees the smooth unfolding of the big picture and considers how it is affected by the details.

Her symbol is found in the writings of many ancient cultures and is the symbol for water or flow. The flow of the unfolding of the purpose of indwelling life is smooth only when seen over the long haul. If we cannot see the perfection of the large picture, the small picture can look very chaotic. Hay-leem-a holds the large vision of how the movement of the river of life will flow in order to guide life back if it veers off course.

"The changes which break up at short intervals the prosperity of men are advertisements of a nature whose law is growth ... And yet the compensations of calamity are made apparent to the understanding also, after long intervals of time."

Essay on the Law of Compensation, Ralph Waldo Emerson

10. **Ur-u-Ama**–'Ur' is light in the Naga language (the sacred language of ancient Lemuria). Her name means Mother of Light. She is also the mother of creativity, artistry and new thought. Her symbol is a weaving, as she brings artistry to the weaving of life. She is the muse that inspires and the dream weaver that turns dreams into manifestation.

Wherever we encounter beauty that fills us with joy, we have just caught a glimpse of the perfection of indwelling life peeping through the mirrors of material life–this is art. The quality is found not only in nature but in all great art. For us a peephole has been opened into that which transcends mortality; something intangible yet eternal. This is the gift of Ur-u-ama, the mother that lets the light shine through into the density.

This goddess brings inspiration to the areas of the web of life that need to be stimulated into creativity; areas that are stagnant, for creativity draws in life-force. Like the epitome of all goddess energy, she enhances the quality of the journey of life.

When an artist goes through a dark night of the soul, it is reflected in his work. His heart isn't in it and so the magic is gone. This goddess withdraws her inspiration from those whose hearts are not in their work; who perform their tasks in mindless drudgery. The product of such work has no soul and is of little benefit to the recipient. The most menial tasks become acts of creativity and devotion when done from the heart.

11. **Amaraku**–'Ama' is mother, 'Ra' means father and 'Ku' is the kundalini or sacred fire energy (also called the serpent energy). Her name stands for the birth of the new. The ku is birthed by the mother and father coming into balance.

The Kumaras (her god counterparts) and the Amarakus, rulers, high priests and priestesses of ancient Lemuria, were naguals. A nagual is a specific type of being that has a double luminous cocoon around their bodies, rather than the usual one that others have (the total shape of all seven bodies stacked inside one another). The purpose for this is to give the nagual more energy so that he or she can fulfill the purpose of their existence; to lead others to freedom from illusion.

Between the second (God-consciousness) and the third (Ascended Mastery) stages of their evolution, naguals' luminous cocoons split and they either become four-pronged or three-pronged naguals, depending on whether it split in two or in three. The four-pronged nagual man and woman work together. He brings information in from the unknown and she births it into new ways of being in the known (material life).

The three-pronged naguals (men and women) become the divine hemaphrodites, representing the neutral element. They bring information in from the unknowable which ideally is interpreted by the four-pronged nagual man and nagual woman into everyday life. The Kumaras and the Amarakus fell into these categories.

The essence of this goddess is to bring in new ways of being– new beginnings. She finds new ways to help expand awareness into the unknown and helps turn it into the known through experience–as do naguals.

The symbol of the three-petalled lotus flower is representative of the way a three-pronged nagual's field splits and also represents the relationship between the three-pronged nagual and nagual man and nagual woman. The lotus flower was one of the symbols for Lemuria, though usually depicted with seven petals. Three stands for the unknowable and also the goddess. It also represents the perfect balance between the masculine, the feminine and the neutral.

12. **Alu-Mi-Na**–'Alu' means of everyone, 'mi' is consciousness and 'na' is wisdom. This word also later became the root for illuminated. Alu-mi-na holds the wisdom of the consciousness of everyone. One has to be illuminated to pass the gate to the unknowable and the source of all knowledge that she guards. That is why her symbol is a candle of illumination.

When all previous goddess orders have been brought into expression and the god orders have blended with them, we become powerful indeed. She will test us to see how wisely we use this power we've accumulated, for beyond the gate she guards lies immortality. This testing comes only once in a lifetime and may take any form and come without a moment's notice.

Her candle fits into the chalice of her god counterpart, symbolizing that they are the last to join before the third and final stage eliminates all thinking and the highest mind takes over.

Alu-mi-na urges self-examination, celebration of accomplishment and deep meaningful living. The lighting of candles during celebration is a remnant from our far distant past when humanity was familiar with this goddess and her aspect of creating celebration along the journey of life.

13. **A-Ra-Ka-Na**–Her name means 'Of Light, Energy and Wisdom'. Her symbol is a stylized spider in the form of a figure eight. The figure eight represents the point of convergence (the zero point) between Creator and Creation. Like the spider sit-

ting in the middle of her web, Ara-ka-na is at the center of all levels of Creation–zero point. All the frequency bands of Creator and Creation meet at this portal, the place of no frequency.

Everything that exists, even something as vast as the Infinite, has the ability to become something more, propelled by the movement of awareness. Zero point is the portal through which new levels of evolution can be accessed.

When we move into the final stage of ascended mastery, the central portal (place of no frequency) within our DNA opens up and we access the energy of all that lies without. Like the cosmic zero point, our DNA becomes the portal between Creator and Creation; we become the I Am that I Am.

The goddess Ara-ka-na holds the potential of that which is waiting to become and like her symbol, Arachne, holds the web of all life that is.

The God Orders

(See Figure 21, 12 God Orders)

1. **La-U-Mi-El**–'La' means all; 'U' a means of; 'Mi' means consciousness and 'El' means Lord (it can also mean "matter"). The name therefore shows that this god is the lord of the consciousness of all. His symbol is the hieroglyph for reciprocity. Its shape comes from an old harvesting device, but it is also a stylized depiction of one hand giving and one receiving.

   As the Goddess Pana-tura manifests material life, La-u-mi-el determines how much consciousness the form should hold by weighing its role within the big picture. An example of this would be: Planets have different ages (called Yugas by the Hindus) they go through based on the light beam from the central sun they are moving through. Some ages, like the one

12 God Orders

1. LA-U-MI-EL Lord of all consciousness. The symbol is the hieroglyph for reciprocity, also used to indicate wisdom in harvesting. This lord works with the law of compensation in nature to bring about the balanced evolution of species.

2. AKASHA-EL Lord of the Akashic records and keeper of history. He is also the keeper of the spoken word and language. He determines the insights of history by being the holder of the big picture. The symbol means permanent record.

3. KARAMA Lord of karma. He determines where karma can best be learned and experienced. The symbol stands for the opening of all 12 chakras, which only occurs when a being has removed the seals of unresolved karma by learning the lessons past experience teaches.

4. URI-EL Lord of intelligence. He is the interpreter of insights gained and redesigns the evolution of awareness accordingly. He turns information through intelligence into the known.

5. KI-AS-MUS Lord of time and space. He works within the allotted amount of time to evolve awareness within a certain space (in Creation, time and space have established limits).

6. MI-RA-EL Lord of symbols of hidden knowledge (includes DNA coding). He determines what must be hidden and what must be revealed within DNA coding or through symbols. He also works with pivotal energy.

7. OM-KA-EL Lord who holds the vision. He creates the template that fulfills the purpose of a certain part of creation. The symbol stands for focus and will, or focused intent.

8. KA-PA-EL Lord of the cycles. He works with the cycles of change all life goes through: transformation, transmutations, and transfiguration. The spiral is either positive, resulting in a higher form of the lifeform, or negative, resulting in death.

9. LEEM-U-EL Lord of the flow of awareness. He oversees the interaction of the different forms of awareness during the in-breath and out-breath of God—the large creational cycles.

10. ILLUMINATI Lord of illumination. He creates the grid lines along which creation will be formed. He is the architect and engineer for wielding sacred geometry.

11. KU-MA-RA Lord of hierarchy and government. He brings stability through structure to growth. He represents the perfect balance between the neutral, feminine and masculine elements.

12. KA-LI-SA Lord of energy distribution. He determines the amount of energy a lifeform can hold.

(Figure 21)

we've just entered, are times of awakening. Others are times of falling asleep.

Once it is determined that an age of forgetfulness is bringing too much darkness to a planet, it becomes necessary to send in a way-shower; a being of great consciousness to get the planetary evolution back on track. Christ was such a way-shower. In order for his body to be of a high enough frequency to house so much consciousness, the Essene lineage had to prepare to receive him for seven generations to receive him. With each subsequent generation the bodies became purer and housed more consciousness.

Within the scenario of Christ's mission, there also had to be a Pontius Pilate and a Herod. They had to have less conscious-ness or the scenario of the crucifixion could not have taken place to survive through the ages as a testimony of the surren-dering of the will to the divine plan.

When we speak of the consciousness an individual is born with, we are speaking in this context of how large or how small a portion of light he or she contains; how 'awake' he or she is. It really means how much of the Infinite's light they reflect.

The other aspect of this great lord is reciprocity. How the level of consciousness a being can contain and reciprocity relate has historically been understood by indigenous cultures. If one receives a gift (the fruit from an apple tree, for example) with awareness of the miracle of its life and gratitude to be able to receive it, the consciousness of the apple tree increases. Through acknowledgement we lead another life form into a higher evolution and more complex expression of life. It is the indigenous way to leave a token gift, like cornmeal or tobacco, as reciprocity to express their gratitude.

Another way in which reciprocity enhances consciousness is

seen in the way we reverse roles lifetime after lifetime. Soul families, usually a group of five whose destinies are connected, often alternate roles in order to maximize each other's opportunities for learning. In one life one may be a perpetrator, and the victim in the next. Civilizations will do the same, hence the rise and fall of empires. This lord orchestrates this.

2. **Akasha-el**–Akasha-el's symbol means permanent record and his name (aka=word, sha=awareness or holy, el=lord) means the lord that holds the awareness of the word. He is the record keeper of the Akashic records; the history keeper of Creation. He looks at the large perspective to gain the insights history offers.

   The Akashic records are like the library of the cosmos. An advanced race facing certain problems, would research the history of another in order to evaluate how they dealt with similar problems. They would do this by accessing the Akashic records, since that race may have existed a billion years ago.

   The Akashic records have three layers–much like a library may have three floors or stories. The bottom story has the records of all experiential knowledge. The middle story has the preserved records of all thoughts that have been thought. The top story has the record of wishes and suppositions. Every time someone thinks, "What would happen if …?" that thought would be stored in this level of the Akashic records.

   When this outbreath of God, this Creational cycle, is concluded, it is Akasha-el who will turn the key of the library over to the Primary Trinity that all insights may be extracted from experience.

3. **Karama**–Karma is a mirror held up for insights to be gained. Our feeling of being victimized is the effect of not understanding this concept or how impossible injustice really is. As the

god of karma, Karama, and the goddess counterpart Ka-li-ma are lived in everyday life, the illusion of injustice is dispelled. The stark truth that we are creators of our own reality becomes irrefutable.

Karma is formed when distorted vision creates distorted emotion. When the mirror of our flawed perception is held up in our environment, our experiences provide us the opportunity to correct our vision.

Unresolved karma constricts the flow of universal energy. This manifests as plugs or seals in our chakras. As we have seen, twelve chakras eventually open as we release these plugs through gaining the insights of our experience. This releases us from karma and opens up a field of light around the body in the shape of a dove. The Lord Karama's sign is the dove, representing the field of a being who has resolved all past karma.

Karama balances individual, national, racial, galactic and cosmic karma. He determines when lessons can best be learned and how the mirrors can be presented to maximize learning.

4. **Uri-el**–Uri-el is the lord of intelligence. Intelligence analyzes and chooses between that which is life-enhancing and that which is not (the choice everything boils down to). He can be regarded as the critic in the audience who watches the play of Creation unfold and gauges the deeper meaning the play is revealing.

His responsibility is to interpret the non-cognitive information (feelings) of the cosmos collected by his goddess counterpart, Ori-ka-la. Many species, such as plant life, explore the unknown through feeling without the ability to interpret those feelings. Since all species have one common goal, the exploration of the unknown, Uri-el and his legions of workers have to interpret this non-cognitive information so that the evolution of awareness can be realigned accordingly.

In addition, the insights from Ascended Masters that are uploaded directly to the Infinite filter down to Creation, changing truth moment by moment. This too needs to be taken into consideration as the initial design for experience may no longer be relevant.

The symbol for Uri-el represents the linear movement of inherent awareness away from Source, since he is realigning the way awareness unfolds. It also represents the four directions, or building blocks of Creation.

5. **Ki-as-mus**–from his name comes the word for cosmos as found in the more modern earth languages. The root for Ki-as-mus or cosmos is the ancient Lemurian word Kia, which means 'x' or partnership (and in later dialects, reflection).

This lord's symbol is an 'x', representing the concept of 'as above, so below'. It also resembles an hourglass to indicate there is only so much allotted time and space for this creational cycle. In order for Creation to expand within a certain space within a certain time, Ki-as-mus needs to regulate the speed with which it unfolds.

To be able to regulate the speed of the evolution of awareness, this lord must regulate stagnation and flow, or growth. Stagnation occurs when beings do not fulfill their contract with the Infinite to explore the unknown by extracting the insights from their experience.

When growth is too slow, Ki-as-mus orchestrates assistance from the 'system-busters' within the cosmos–beings of light who, through great self sacrifice, rapidly descend to dense areas and incarnate there to become the way-showers.

When growth is too rapid, the corresponding goddess Aubari brings some of Lucifer's rage to be taken on, based on Ki-as-mus's calculations as to how much the growth needs to be retarded. Souls then volunteer to take on Lucifer's rage in order to change it into understanding.

6. **Mi-ra-el**–This god archetype works in conjunction with Ki-as-mus to infuse certain portions of Creation with light. For instance, if all of humanity entered into God-consciousness today, it would be disastrous for many races whose lessons we are vicariously learning, since learning slows dramatically during the first two phases of God-consciousness. The Lord Mi-ra-el therefore programs codes into the human DNA that will only activate our ability to receive more light when certain lessons are learned.

The other method to activate a higher level of awareness at the expedient moment is to provide symbols or codes representing hidden bodies of information. When confronted with that code or symbol at a specific time, the memory of the information it represents returns. If humankind is responsible for solving the mystery of relationship, for example, it is necessary that we forget we are all one. Relating would otherwise be impossible. In this way, Mi-ra-el decides what can be revealed and what must remain hidden to fulfill the overall purpose.

This lord's symbol is a DNA strand because of his key role in programming DNA. There is a deeper meaning to the symbol, though, that reveals a further facet of his overall purpose.

The DNA strands do not in fact cross over the way it would appear as a two-dimensional symbol. They twist or pivot and only appear to be crossing over each other. Like his goddess counterpart, this lord works with pivotal energy. Whereas her responsibility is to reverse the flow of events going in an undesirable direction, his is to provide those key moments that turn life into a new and enhanced direction.

All great spiritual traditions have taught that huge changes into higher awareness hinge on these key moments. The Taoist traditions say: The dawn comes but once. Toltec training focuses on preparing the apprentice for that moment of testing that comes but once to see if he or she is worthy of breaking free from mortal boundaries.

When designing an individual's key moments, Mi-ra-el must determine the exact timing when the degree of readiness has been reached by that individual. The pivotal moment must be filled with symbolism programmed into his DNA pertinent to his destiny. It has to be relevant to that which he has contracted with the Infinite to solve.

7. **Om-Ka-El**–The symbol for this god is a tetrahedron inside a sphere. The sphere stands for mind (om), and will or fire (ka) is represented by the tetrahedron.

When the god orders decide that certain insights have failed to yield themselves in spite of many beings attempting to extract them through experience, Om-ka-el designs an experimental template where these issues can be focused upon. An example is the loop of time on which humanity has been traveling.

Because the races have to be in a state of unity within diversity for this outbreath to come to a timely conclusion, the future dynasty or template was designed by Om-ka-el. Since it failed to reach the desired result, an additional template, namely humanity on a loop in time, was designed to explore its missing insights.

Once the template is designed, Om-ka-el has to hold the space for completion of the experiment. Because of how much responsibility rests upon humanity, there have been focused attempts to either repress or eliminate us altogether. There have also been well-meaning attempts to 'enlighten' the entire race by other races who do not see the big picture and fail to recognize the value of humanity's folly.

Om-ka-el regulates that for every suppression, a balancing amount of light is let in so that the overall result is one of non-interference. He has to prevent deluded ones from destroying those involved in the experiment. The earth has had to come under stringent protection from this god because of its role as the pivot point for the future.

The assistance from his goddess counterpart, Ishana-ma, helps dissimilar components within an experiment (like the races on earth) interact more smoothly.

8. **Ka-pa-el**–The god Ka-pa-el's symbol is one commonly used in electronics and is also found in crop glyphs that have appeared in recent years. In electronics it stands for 'capacitor' which can be described as a storage unit for energy. A capacitor for energy is like a jug for water–one can store enough for later use by holding it under the tap.

Races, planetary systems or individuals can hold only so much energy in their present form just as the jug can hold only so much water. If the volume of energy becomes too great, it must transfigure to the next level of its evolution. If the energy volume is too low, it must recycle itself (die). Ka-pa-el monitors these cycles.

His name means the parent of energy. This symbol of a capacitor is relevant for other reasons as well: He himself is a capacitor in that he stores energy released when a material form dies and releases it again when that being takes on another body. From the smallest pansy in the garden to the death and rebirth of solar systems, Ka-pa-el is the steward of energy released or needed during these cycles.

It is this principle of the capacitor that awakens life within the

Infinite as it gains more and more insight and energy and finally has to transfigure. The release of energy when 'the jug finally overflows' is what awakens the Infinite's emotions.

9. **Leem-u-el**–The god Leem-u-el has a symbol representing the tube torus, the great movement of the inbreath and outbreath of God. The top of his symbol is yellow and the bottom is black, representing the day and night of Creation; the time of waking up and falling asleep; the outbreath and inbreath.

His name means Lord of the Flow and his concerns are the big cycles of Creation. He holds the vision of destiny for all life–that contract we made with the Infinite as to what portion of the unknown we will solve with all our multiple lives. He oversees how personal destinies contribute to the fulfilling of the cosmic destiny. The cosmic destiny is the overall sum of the contracts or goals for this outbreath of God. Each outbreath has a very specific purpose to accomplish, adding to the perception gained by preceding cycles until the Vast Being which includes Creation, transfigures itself.

Leem-u-el takes into consideration which parts of the overall plan are still undone and gives this information to other gods to design or re-design templates or to consider as they design timing or the speed with which the plan unfolds. It helps the Lord Karama determine how much pain is needed to prod change.

10. **Illuminati**–The name of this sacred god order must not be confused with any group on earth calling themselves by this name or using this sacred symbol. Those who have had access to pieces of hidden knowledge they have wished to use to gain power have frequently patterned themselves after these eternal truths. The lord of Illuminati (lord of the illuminated ones) has a right eye as his symbol because it is governed by left brain knowledge. He illuminates with information.

Around each planet stacked grids or meshes of lines of light govern the species of the planet. Each species has its own grid telling it how to behave. The more complex the expression of the species, the higher up the grid is 'stacked', forming a hierarchy of species in terms of complexity. The lord of Illuminati is responsible for programming the grids and energy lines so that each species can play its appropriate part in the grand design of Creation.

Just as the three original, highest bodies of the vast being in which we dwell (the Mother of God) had aspects of itself 'fall' in consciousness to produce first the Infinite and then Creation, so a planet falls in consciousness until it is fully physical. Each time a planet or a solar system falls, this lord needs to re-program the grids to accommodate the lower consciousness as it transfigures.

11. **Ku-ma-ra**–We have discussed the way these orders functioned in ancient Lemuria under the corresponding goddess. In the cosmos, however, the function of the god Ku-ma-ra is to step down information which is light from one band of compassion to the next. The symbol stands for the four bands of compassion within Creator and Creation as represented by the Hebrew letters yod, hay, vau, hay. They appear inside a banner as used by the Lemurian rulers.

The order in the cosmos is due to the orders of the cosmos. In other words, throughout the cosmos a hierarchy of government exists that receives guidance in the form of information from higher up to interpret for levels lower down. These rulers or kings are the Ku-ma-ras. The god Ku-ma-ra relays the loftiest levels of information from one band of compassion to the next.

The three sides of the banner also represent the relationship among the three-pronged nagual, the four-pronged nagual man and the four-pronged nagual woman. In the government of the cosmos this governing trinity is found at every level.

In ancient earthly civilizations the rulers were the ones with the greatest vision and wisdom. As earth fell in consciousness, the rulers were often the most ruthless or the most powerful. The principle of the Ku-ma-ras acting as a conduit for higher guidance for the people became obscured and darkness and pain replaced the golden ages. The parents or rulers (Ku stands for energy directed from the Ma or mother, and Ra or father) began exploiting their charges or children.

12. **Ka-li-sa**–Ka is energy or sacred fire. Li means to illuminate and Sa means holy (as in Saint) or awareness. Lisa, in later dialects of the old mother tongue, means container. Ka-li-sa means container of sacred fire. The word 'chalice' comes from Ka-li-sa.

This god's symbol is a chalice. The candle symbol of the corresponding goddess, Alu-mi-na, can stand within the chalice. The merging of their symbols is significant in that they are the last pair of god and goddess archetypes to merge (which must occur before Ara-ka-na can open the portal to the next cycle of evolution).

The god Ka-li-sa is the lord of initiation and prepares the recipient to be able to contain more light or a higher level of light. Light travels along pathways the way water travels along rivers. If a dam bursts upstream, the river can no longer accommodate this increased amount of water and floods over its banks. In a similar way, initiations assist in preparing the nervous system to receive a greater amount of light.

The principle applies throughout the cosmos. If a planet is transfiguring, its ley lines and planetary grids need to be changed to accommodate the resulting increase in light.

The function of this god is an essential component of preparing to enter through the portal of Ara-ka-na into a new cycle of evolution. The largest leap in consciousness any being can make is to move from the stages of one form of expression of awareness to the next. Many have tried to leave the stages of humanity without proper preparation with dire results, especially among Toltec seers (most other traditions don't make it this far). If we have earned the right to cross beyond this point, the level of light we have achieved will be gauged by Almu-mi-na to be sufficient, Ka-li-sa will prepare us for what lies beyond and we will exit the human kingdom and enter the god kingdom.

CHAPTER FOUR

THE ALCHEMY OF RELATIONSHIP

Relationship–Sacred Key to Unlocking the Mysteries of God

When the One expresses as the many through its creations, it is for the purpose of learning about the mysteries of its being. This is done by the many parts relating and mirroring various facets of existence to one another. The Infinite itself is increasing in knowledge and light, which is information, through relationship–the relationship with its Creation. (See Figure 22, Blueprint of Social and Relationship Stages)

Relationship can therefore be regarded as the Holy of Holies, the sacred inner temple where the purpose of the Infinite is fulfilled. With each relationship a new opportunity is presented to unlock another of the mysteries of God's being that have never been accessed before. It is the sacred cauldron of alchemy where

171

Blueprint of Social and Relationship Stages

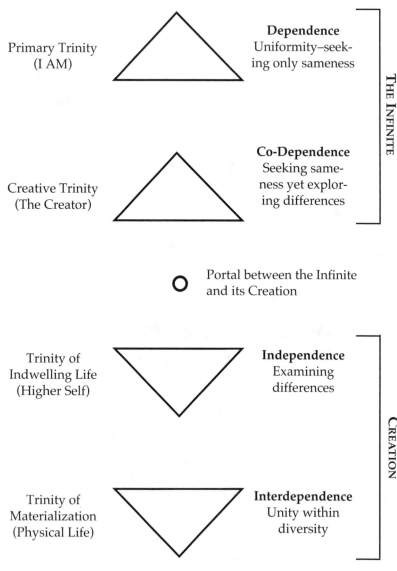

(Figure 22)

lead (the unknown or unyielded light) becomes gold (the known or light). The gift of relationship can never be taken for granted.

Although all relationships mirror to us that which we are, that which we judge, that which we've lost or that which we have yet to learn, few of us take the time to observe the profound lessons they bring. As we grow in awareness, we find our hearts opening to include all life and at that point we not only learn from the mirrors in our own experience, but also by observing others.

It is an act of unconditional love not to let the experience of others pass fruitlessly by. In gaining insights on their behalf, we can lift them off their treadmill through our compassion. Life will now allow them to move on to solving other parts of the mystery rather than repeat the same experiences over and over.

Relationship is the primary tool in the evolution of awareness. When a relationship stagnates, forced change breaks the stalemate. The two primary causes of this stagnation are: first, when relationship does not evolve through its stages of growth, and second, when an imbalance exists within its polarity. In other words, stagnation occurs when its masculine and feminine components persist in being grossly imbalanced. The gift of imbalance is growth. If all things are in perfect balance, there is no movement in awareness. When imbalance persists on one side or another, however, stagnation occurs.

The evolutionary stages of relationship are the same for interpersonal or cultural relationships. (See Figure 22,Blueprint of Social and Relationship Stages)

1. **Dependence:** In this stage similarities are stressed. Couples experience this as their initial stage of being 'in love'. They feel euphoric because they see themselves in the mirror of the other person. Culturally this manifests as tribal life where the individual is expected to behave in a certain way in exchange for the tribe's support.

2. **Co-dependence:** Some individuality is expressed, but there is still a strong desire to identify with each other and no-one steps too far out of 'the box'. Many tribal members in North America are in this stage, where they live in the city, but retain strong ties of dependence with the tribe.

3. **Independence:** In personal interaction each individual becomes almost desperate to find his or her own identity. Differences now become emphasized. In the modern, mechanized societies all types of insurance are needed since there is no tribal support. In apartments people live without knowing their neighbor's name.

4. **Interdependence:** If stage 3 can be survived, this stage brings more stability. The individuals are secure in their relationships, and supportive of each others' differences. This is the template for communal living for the future: a group lives together because of a common goal, voluntarily commits certain contributions and is free to express and grow in diversity.

These stages lead from uniformity to unity within diversity. Uniformity cannot fully embody the will of the Infinite to explore beingness through its creations. There's less commitment to the larger picture and self-centeredness can develop. In the stage of unity within diversity the chances are maximized for individual growth to contribute to the growth of the group within a stable environment. Tribal societies that remaining in sameness are painfully pushed into change. Diversity produces more chances of exploring the unknown.

When partners do not bring an inner balance of masculine and feminine to a relationship, but rely instead on the other partner to provide the missing piece, the relationship is at risk. The minute one partner gains better inner balance, the other partner no longer knows how to relate.

In the same way nations and races become vulnerable when, for instance, the feminine within them isn't allowed full and proper expression. There are feminine cultures on earth that have deep intrinsic spirituality that permeates everyday life and masculine societies where logic, science, and materialism pervade.

Cultures that have been conquered such as Tibet, indigenous peoples in North and South America, the Jewish, Armenian and others, epitomize the feminine conquered by the masculine. This mirrors the inner imbalance brought about when the spiritual aspects of that culture have been dominated by males and in some instances have excluded the feminine

Relationship is part of the most powerful force in existence: the desire of the Infinite to evolve its awareness. As such, it is unstoppable in its purpose to promote growth. We can either honor it, co-operating with its divine mission to explore consciousness, or become its casualty. We are never a victim; the choice always has been and always will be ours.

Responsibility–Supporting Versus Saving

One of the greatest impediments to the progress of light workers is a misplaced sense of responsibility–the misguided and deep seated feeling that we need to feel guilty about flourishing when another does not. We often seem to think that somehow we serve life best when we join others in their blind victimhood, or that we dare not be happy until we have saved others.

We view happiness as something we must deserve, rather than the birthright of man. Instead of letting our light shine and becoming one of the way-showers or light beacons of the planet, we sink back into the misery of man. Wearing the ball and chain of guilt and the need to save, we are prevented from flying upon the high winds of destiny.

When we embark upon the path of enlightenment, we must release others to the responsibility of their higher divine selves. With the exception of our responsibility to our minor children, we are responsible only for ourselves. If we can unfold into our godhood, we can raise the consciousness of every man, women, and child on earth. Our greatest contribution always is through the altered frequency we emit as we become filled with light and not through what we do. This pure frequency changes all it touches.

To be responsible only for one's self is the core of an attitude that refuses to save those who manipulate through ineptness. Manipulation by those who shirk taking responsibility for their own life can include the following:

- Confusion–Confusion and obsessing about the questions is a choice, and as long as others (who not feeling lovable, settle for feeling needed) are around to save us, we do not need to develop self reliance;
- Self-destructiveness–If I find no value in my own life, but you keep trying to rescue me, it must have value. Also, if I have not dealt with feeling unloved by parents, I place you in a saving parent role which makes me feel loved;
- Keep me from feeling pain–Pain is the desire for change. If we keep someone from feeling pain, we also keep them from change. Through indulging them we inadvertently keep them in their agony. The key is to organize instead of agonize; to help construct a way out of that which needs to be changed is better than wallowing in the pain until it becomes a 'trusted' companion;
- The Blame Game–If I can get you to feel guilty, you will keep trying to compensate, making me able to control you. Or if I rage at you and keep you off balance by continually having to defend yourself, I have you hooked into my game.

Responsibilities we cannot shirk are:

- Our fiduciary responsibility to minor children;
- Responsibilities we have contracted to perform, such as a job we undertake to perform where others rely on our fulfilling it;
- To speak our highest wisdom when asked for it or when a situation presents itself where it is needed;
- The responsibility not to abuse a parental/counselor role we undertake that provides the opportunity for another to become vulnerable (the reason why a psychologist or spiritual counselor cannot have a sexual relationship with a client);
- To lend a helping hand when we have the capability to help another out of a crisis or a 'stuck' place in order to move to a higher order.

Misplaced senses of responsibility:

- We are not responsible for saving someone on an ongoing basis if their conduct indicates they are not prepared to help themselves and they keep returning to their old mode of conduct;
- We are not required to sacrifice our ability to evolve and thrive in order to spare another's feelings;
- We are not responsible for shielding others from looking at their own short-comings by making excuses for, or compensating for them;
- We are not responsible for dimming our light so others can feel better about themselves. If we all sank to the level of the lowest common denominator, there would be none to inspire and amaze us; no one to give us vision of what the human race can achieve or fill us with hope of transcending our limited self.

Our primary responsibility is to fulfill the purpose of our creation; that contract we made with the Infinite to pierce the mystery of beingness with light and fold back the boundaries of darkness, illuminating with compassionate understanding even the darkest recesses of Creation.

Stalkers Versus Dreamers

For the cosmos to come to a resolution enabling it to return to the heart of God on the inbreath, it has to achieve something similar to a human being preparing for entry into God-consciousness. The left and right 'brain functions', or way of accessing reality, have to blend and work smoothly together.

The right and left 'brains' of the cosmos are represented by the left and right brain races. One of the biggest challenges that must be met is for these races to cooperate and successfully interact. Because the earth is the arena in which many of the cosmic problems are solved, humanity consists of both left- brained and right-brained dominant individuals.

The planet is feminine and the right-brain oriented people outnumber the left-brain dominant ones (we shall call the right-brained ones Dreamers and the left-brained people Stalkers). Those approaching life through the left brain, the Stalkers, have what is called a vertical approach to life. The right-brained Dreamers approach life horizontally.

The reason for this description is that, at the moment awareness is born (when the implosion occurs), the mental component of the Infinite, which is a vertical wave form, fuses with the emotional horizontal wave form. Awareness consists of both wave forms, horizontal and vertical, fused together as two carrier waves traveling together. A cross section would look like a wobbly cross.

The Stalkers access more of the vertical mental waves of awareness and the Dreamers the horizontal waves. Stalkers access the known deeply and analytically, like a flashlight shining a small, bright, clearly defined lightbeam onto a wall. Dreamers access more of the unknown, like a circle of wide, diffused light. Stalkers can juggle twelve balls in the external world for every one the Dreamers can. But Dreamers will pick up many times more non-cognitive information.

The way Dreamers access the world has been very much misunderstood. The educational system is designed around the way Stalkers think. As it is, Stalkers can grasp external information at the rate of thirty-four units to every twenty-one units the Dreamers can. The Dreamers have consequently traditionally been underestimated and under-achieving.

Because we are archetypically finding a way for the cooperation of these two dissimilar parts of Creation to take place, we are manifesting personal relationships in which to study these approaches:

Stalkers in Relationships

- In personal relationships Dreamers find Stalkers cold and calculating at times. They are less inclined to make small talk and think they're helping by analyzing their partners or the situation.
- Stalkers often fire facts at co-workers or employees in a way that reminds one of a machine gun. They may pause for breath just long enough to ask whether there are any questions, since they may be getting a dazed look from the Dreamer listeners. However, the Dreamers can't assimilate such a deluge of information, get lost early in the conversation and don't even know at this point what the questions are.
- Stalkers feel unheard because after 'carefully explaining' in great detail, it's clear that nobody seems to do as instructed (since no one understood).
- Stalkers may ask Dreamers a question (since they seldom make

179

small talk, it's abstract or profound) and get unclear or evasive answers. Again they feel unheard, not understanding that Dreamers will process a question by internalizing it; feeling it in their heart. Only then will they think it over. It could take days.

• Stalkers feel particularly unheard when voicing their feelings. A typical conversation between a Stalker husband and a Dreamer wife may go as follows:

The husband comes home from work and complains that the lunch she makes him every day is giving him heartburn. She is washing the dishes, hardly looks up and says, "That's nice, dear. By the way, the upstairs toilet is plugged. Would you fix it?" He thinks she doesn't care, but what she has really said is that it's not the lunch; his 'plumbing' is backed up. She doesn't know herself what her words mean. She just accesses it. He's supposed to analyze it.

Dreamers in Relationships

• Dreamers feel unheard by Stalkers. The Stalkers find Dreamers' questions to be out of place, not on track, or not to the point. They are therefore often dismissed as not contributing or being irrelevant.

• When Dreamers express their feelings, it's often very emotional and appears to the frustrated Stalker to be irrational or illogical. When a Stalker husband tries to create order out of his Dreamer wife's 'ramblings', she feels he is not honoring the process of her feelings.

There are great gifts Stalkers and Dreamers can give each other. The Dreamers have a knack for improving the quality of the journey through life. They may take longer to reach the goal, but the end product is often more creative. They provide a lot of energy to Stalkers through their association.

Stalkers are goal-minded and bring organization to the Dreamer's life. They are good at running daily life and creating order out of chaos, something that appeals to Dreamers who frequently have difficulty keeping the physical aspects of their life in order.

Until Dreamers and Stalkers see how to utilize the respective gifts each mindset brings to the relationship, the friction between these groups will be ongoing. Many of us still look for uniformity in our relationships, which brings stagnation rather than growth. The goal of having unity within diversity promotes the most growth but requires understanding, patience and the tolerance necessary to support each other's differences.

How Stalkers and Dreamers Can Bridge the Communication Gap

If the two different camps want to communicate they will have to learn each other's skill sets.

Tools for Dreamers

• Dreamers can be seen as slow since, as previously discussed, their ratio of assimilating new information is twenty-one to thirty-four in respect to Stalkers. It will assist them to cultivate the tool of speed-reading. Colleges offer classes in this.

• Dreamers get overwhelmed when bombarded by information. They either need to take a proper shorthand class or develop their own shorthand system.

• Dreamers hold long term memory patterns well, but not short term memory. They have to cultivate better short term memory by practicing with pieces of information they can afford to fail with. Read a phone number once, dial the whole number; do the same with an address. When typing something on the computer, try to type longer and longer pieces without looking at notes.

• When given complex instructions, use shorthand. Then take time to digest and sort out what has been said. See if there are any gaps in the information and them formulate concise, but comprehensive questions to obtain the missing pieces and do not be afraid to ask.

• Remember always that Stalkers will hold you accountable for every word you say.

Tools for Stalkers

• Stalkers should identify the Dreamers in their environment and slow down the instructions or conversation by using metaphors, examples, stories and humor. When Stalkers are speaking too fast, Dreamers cannot ask questions since they do not even know what to ask.

• Stalkers must remember that Dreamers could be more intelligent than they are perceived to be, but that the system has not allowed them to shine. Remember too, most people are Dreamers.

• Stalkers have often become impatient with Dreamers and by now the Dreamers tend to shut down when Stalkers get confrontational, or blaming or 'controlling'.

• Stalkers will isolate themselves from others unless they loosen their expectations. By being over-focused on results they can alienate the rest of the team. Remember, Dreamers view time differently. Those speaking vowel-oriented languages (such as aboriginal peoples) have world-views that are even more relaxed about hurrying through life. When I started speaking star language, my concept of time changed instantly.

• Stalkers need to have what to them seems like 'meaningless social interaction' in order to get Dreamers to relax around them so that the Stalkers can be heard. If the Stalker has a Dreamer boss, social co-workers may be promoted over him, because of the value Dreamers place on the quality of the journey.

• Stalkers must remember that most Dreamers say things they don't mean when emotional. They should at least try and listen behind the words to their intent, using the heart rather than the head. Ask a few questions when the emotions are spent (too many will make Dreamers feel interrogated). Developing listening skills is the number one skill for Stalkers to cultivate in trying to bridge the gap.

Sacred Sexuality

There is only one criterion for weighing our actions: do they serve indwelling life or don't they. If they serve the world of form only, they serve that which is unreal. On the other hand, if actions serve to evolve awareness, then they are aligned with the purpose of indwelling life.

The degree to which sexual acts are enhancing to the indwelling life of participants depends on the consciousness that initiates them. To be conscious is to see the big picture. Conscious beings consider carefully the effects of any act on others. They know that any choice they make must benefit all equally in the evolution of awareness.

Many sexual 'spiritual' practices are designed to enhance energy, which in turn increases consciousness, but not always equally to both participants. Using another to enhance primarily one's own energy can provide short-term energy boosts but will ultimately deplete not only oneself, but also one's environment. A practice that focuses on self-gain is self-centered, a condition that de-spirals the DNA strand and warps the web of existence, creating karmic repercussions.

The ancient Chinese traditions of the White Tigress women enabled practitioners to remain youthful into their nineties and beyond through the energy these practices provided. Like vampires of energy, there was personal gain to them with little exchange. Tantric practices provide more of an exchange, yet are nevertheless more enhancing to males.

There is a limited amount of power and energy available from the form side of life and a limitless supply from the Divine that breathes life into form. The only way to gain energy and power without damaging the web of existence is through enhanced perception. The secret to unlocking the gift of perception that sexuality can yield lies in that place of connection with the Infinite: the present moment. It is in the stillness of the moment that we experience the ultimate love affair between Creator and Creation. It can be demonstrated in the following way: if we pass blindly by a flowering bush along the wayside and fail to see that it is ablaze with the glory of God, nature withers. Nature thrives on appreciation. If in a quiet moment of contemplation, we truly acknowledge the beauty of a flower, it allows that plant to evolve more rapidly into a more complex form of expression.

In a similar way, truly being present and appreciatively entering into the wondrous miracles of our partners, contributes to their evolution of awareness. Thoughts about techniques pull us out of the moment into the world of form and away from indwelling life.

As we focus on truly experiencing another, the energy lines around our bodies open like the radiating petals of a flower. When this happens, blockages are released and power and energy flow freely through us, allowing us to receive a greater supply of life force. Once we shift our focus, however, to personal performance or agendas, the energy lines fold inwards, draining energy from our partners. The energy we drain from another may temporarily increase our own but, as is the case with all self-centeredness, eventually leads to decay and death.

Our insensitivity to the miracle of another disrupts the web of life because it is damaging to them as well as ourselves. It is damaging to them because what is unacknowledged decreases and what is appreciated increases. It is damaging to us because our true identity is a being as vast as the cosmos with all existing within us. What is destructive to another is therefore also destructive to ourselves.

To truly experience another is a matter of the heart. The mind and senses can only appreciate the form, but the heart can know the divine essence within. In this way another being, whether a partner or a flower, becomes a doorway that leads from the world of mirrors (form) into that which is real (indwelling life).

The doorway of the human being reveals a far more complex expression of life than the flower. Creation can be described as a mirror that allows the Infinite to see itself. A human being holds up a larger piece of mirror, revealing more of the Infinite's face than the mirror fragment of the flower. A human being, unlike the flower, has the ability to make mistakes. In this way he also mirrors that which the Infinite is not, that it may more fully understand that which it is.

Each human being is a unique perspective superimposed over all that is. The gift of perception sexual union offers us is that we may enrich ourselves by experiencing another's eternal perspective. When a partner has a lower level of awareness, it becomes more challenging to pierce the illusions (mirrors).

If we approach them superficially, we become entangled in their web of illusions. Through opened hearts we can, on the other hand, see the true perfection of their essence which is why sex and love should go hand in hand. By focusing on the perfection underlying the appearances, we see with the eyes of God. Before such a gaze, illusion dissipates like mist before the morning sun.

The Power of the Spoken Word

The words we speak carry a frequency that pulls in the blueprint creating our reality. They are powerful beyond belief and mold our very existence. Words give us away by revealing the core beliefs we may harbor about ourselves and hope to hide. An aura of glamour can be created around a movie star by those promoters who spin their illusions well, but the minute she opens her mouth the foibles of all her humanness stand revealed.

The birth trauma and early childhood suffering reveal themselves through the shallowness of our breath.[10] We can become as masterful in other areas as we wish but the trauma, held as grief in our lungs, must be released by re-birthing techniques or daily breathing exercises and recapitulation. Perception about why we have come into this density and our true identity as beings of infinite vastness may also cause a spontaneous re-capitulation of birth trauma that can resemble a panic attack accompanied by feelings of grief, desolation and abandonment. Perception is always the method for converting pain to power.

As we grow into the spiritual maturity needed to change humanity's suffering into a joyful participation in life, we are required to take on more responsibility. No longer do we live mindlessly and unconsciously but realize that instead of praying to an 'outside' source to save us, we are the creators of the quality of our journey. Every thought, every word and every deed shapes our

10 See *A Life of Miracles* for breathing techniques to remove these blocks.

lives into either a journey of tragedy or a magical, self-empowering adventure.

The changes in our patterns of speech to those of self-empowerment begin with studying the hidden laws of the spoken word.

- **Words can be living or dead**. This means that words can either be life-altering communications or simply repetitions of the opinions or views of another person. What infuses our words with that spark that brings them to life is the true experiential knowledge behind them or the sincerity of our ideas. Sincerity has an emotional component, a conviction that the words need to be heard. Throughout the ages orators have swayed others by the sincerity of their delivery. Many mistake sincerity for truth. But whether born of truth or simply one person's conviction, words filled with sincerity are alive and sway others.

- **Negative words do not register** on that delicate substance that fills the cosmos and responds to our thoughts and words. This principle is an important one when assessing the true motives of spiritual leaders and channeled entities. If someone is in a spiritually-oriented leadership position, they must have enough intuitive knowledge to judge the effects of their words on others. If their delivery uses negatives to make their points, they are programming into their delivery the opposite of what their listeners hear. "You <u>are</u> not such and such" actually registers as "You are such and such."

- **Self-defeating speech mannerisms** bring about failure in our lives.
    - Not finishing a sentence before breathing (due to birth trauma, hiatal hernia and other causes) does not deliver the statement on the outbreath. This reduces its power and ability to manifest.
    - Phrasing statements as questions or turning the voice up at

the end as though it were a question.

Negating the authority of the statement–"I may be wrong, but..." or by adding diminutives such as, "You're a <u>little</u> grumpy today."

• Pretending to be uncertain. Many highly intelligent people deliberately cultivate a slight stutter in order to be liked by or fit in with others. They feign uncertainty in order to seem non-confrontational.

• If we consider the holy nature of our true identity as a part of the I AM, we want to consider very carefully what words we choose to follow the statement, "I am ...". It is an empowering habit to use only positive words to complete this statement. Even the words "I am sorry" adversely program the subconscious.

• **Sarcasm vs. Irony**

The cosmos functions according to principles based on absolute truth. Every step of the way the grand design has as its purpose the turning of illusion into truth. When we in any way get of out synchronicity with this purpose, life diminishes and conversely, when every action and word is based on truth, life flourishes.

In our search for truth we use the tools of discernment: not-doing and sobriety for the known and dreaming and feeling for the unknown. (See the section on these tools later in the book) Unfortunately the tools can become less effective when our belief systems cause an internal dialog that muddies the waters of our environment. For example, we could feel something to be 'true' because it fits our already held belief systems and something else as not true because it doesn't.

Another obstacle to understanding whether something is true or not is that the advanced souls who have incarnated here for their role in the earth's glorious destiny as the wayshower back to the heart of God, don't know untruth. They have mostly come here from realms beyond illusion and the purity of these souls knows only absolute truth. When confronted with that which we do not have within, the soul recoils and a feeling of confusion drains our energy.

Irony as a figure of speech says what it means but in a sardonic or ironic way. Sarcasm on the other hand says the opposite of what is meant. Both are meant to be used humorously, albeit sometimes at the expense of another.

The cells in the body as miraculous microcosmic replicas of the whole, respond favorably to truth and release lifeforce and energy when untruth is lived or spoken by the body. In the presence of untruth therefore energy is lost and because of its correlation to consciousness, that too is diminished.

In addition, aging of the cells occurs when lifeforce is lost by living in any way out of step with the mission statement of Creation: find and understand truth, even if it is found in the most obscure places in existence. Irony is therefore in harmony with indwelling life and sarcasm, saying the opposite of that which is true, does not. On a path of impeccability where energy is reverently conserved as the wellspring of material life and the foremost requirement for consciousness, sarcasm is either completely eliminated or converted to irony.

Many are addicted to frivolous chatter that keeps them from feeling the emptiness of having abandoned their sub-personalities. Leaking energy in this way keeps us from our mastery. The true warrior is frugal in action and speech and even in the time spent interacting with others.

"Deep in the silence, first ye must linger, until at last
ye are free from desire, free from the longing to

*speak in the silence, conquer by silence, the
bondage of words."*

The Emerald Tablets, Tablet IV

Preliminary Steps in Determining Whether Conflict Exists

If one is walking a path of impeccability, it is imperative to suspend judgment when some seeming offense or disagreement occurs until we have obtained clarity. For example, some acquaintance hurts our feelings, but we realize that words can mislead. We therefore ask, "What did you mean when you said …?" or "Why do you say such and such?" This is not asked in judgment, for no conclusion has been reached, but rather with an attitude of neutrality.

When we have ascertained the true meaning of what was said through feeling the intent behind the words and getting as much clarity as possible, we can proceed. Does it still bring our hackles up or create a knee-jerk reaction? If it does, we need to ask whether it is important enough to resolve with the other person or is it merely one of our 'buttons' that were pushed in order for us to examine some event in our own life that is waiting to yield its insights and power.

If it is important, however, it needs to be addressed. Here are some guidelines on how to decide what is important enough to merit confrontation:

• When there is hurtful intent or destructiveness;
• When it is injurious to the inner child, disrespectful to the sacred world of the inner sage or belittling to the inner nurturer;
• When it violates our privacy or our sacred space;
• When it violates our mutual agreement or trust or is dishonest in any way;

- When it belittles us or suppresses expressing our individuality or causes us to have to be less than we are;
- When it attempts to manipulate, control or dominate us;
- When it criticizes or accuses us.

   If it fits into one of the above or a similar scenario, the following approach should be used:
- First of all some basics should be agreed upon and perhaps even written;
- Within our relationships all feelings are valid (meaning we do not criticize someone for feeling a certain way);
- All emotions should find a safe place for expression;
- Phrases such as "You always", "You never" and "Why do you?" (when the latter is not a question but a disguised accusation) should be prohibited;
- Neither words nor emotions should be used to attack or manipulate.;
- When someone is in the grip of uncontrollable rage, there should be pre-existing coping mechanisms established. They are to wash their face and hands and engage in strenuous activity (exercise bike, jogging, etc.) to organize their thoughts before expressing them;
- Writing letters that are not dispatched is also a productive form of communication where there are rage issues.

   Feelings must be expressed and a solution proposed by the confronting person. This may have to be done a few times before achieving results. "When you do this, I feel this. Is it possible that in future we can try such and such?"

   The appropriate way for the other person to respond is to first make sure they understand. "Are you saying that ...?" If they acknowledge that a change in behavior is appropriate, it is advisable to create a backup plan since deep-seated habits are hard to break. "Can we have a secret hand gesture or phrase to remind you when old habits creep in?" or, "Could I pull you aside to remind you?"

If instead the other person starts venting, sit absolutely still and let it run its course until it is spent. Then repeat what you said, always bringing the conversation back to the relevant point. If this does not work, write it out and request a written response within a few days. If this fails to resolve the issue, the four steps of conflict resolution, discussed later in this chapter, are introduced (in writing if needed).

Should the disagreement persist, there are only three choices remaining:

1. **Evaluate** whether what you have in common contributes sufficiently to your life for you to continue to put up with the differences. If the differences are more significant, either sever the relationship or be prepared for ongoing discomfort;

2. **Flow** around the obstacles because the relationship has been determined to be worth saving. Be creative. He embarrasses you in public? Create a private world for your interaction and make as many public appearances as possible alone. It is never a good idea to force round pegs into square holes;

3. **Change** your attitude. Even if you do the damage control suggested in #2 there are still going to be odd times when the offensive behavior will happen. Lift yourself above the situation like the eagle that flies above the world. Envision yourself sitting in an insulating bubble of pinkish purple light, holding your inner child and talking to it during the occurrence.

It is never to the benefit of indwelling life to accept the unacceptable. It is also eroding to have many 'little' occurrences happen day in and day out. How diligently is the person working on improving him or herself? All these factors must be taken into consideration in coming to a final conclusion. Another helpful tool is to picture enduring this behavior for the next ten years and weigh it against the positive aspects of the relationship.

Conflict Resolution According to the Cosmic Blueprint

As said earlier, it is in the densest levels of Creation where all new knowledge is gained and where life bursts forth in the most astonishing array of diversity in order to maximize the opportunity to successfully fulfill the destiny of all lifeforms and to explore the unknown.

But man is unique among these lifeforms, inspiring in other races of the cosmos both hope and fear. For man, although steeped in illusion, has the almost unfathomable ability to directly shape the unfoldment of the plan of Creation and within our DNA lies key to initiate the in-breath of God; to take the cosmos over the edge of Creation from the 'red road' leading away from the heart of God to the 'blue road' that returns.

In order to be the way-showers for the cosmos, we have been created to represent all kingdoms and races and are a synthesis of all that is within Creation. But because Creation is a mirror of the face of God and we are representative of all Creation, we are that which most fully represents the Infinite. It is as though we hold a large piece of mirror in which the Infinite observes itself, while other creations hold much smaller fragments that reflect smaller portions of the image.

But it is also the sacred duty of man to solve all conflicts that have not yet been brought to resolution. In this way we not only evolve awareness, but as the microcosm of the macrocosm we upload our gained insights directly to the Primary Trinity (the I

193

AM). As a result of this increased perception, the Primary Trinity reflects down to the Creative Trinity (the Creator) an altered message as to what needs to be explored through Creation. The Creative Trinity then injects into the higher aspects of Creation (the Trinity of In-Dwelling Life (or higher self) a change in the way the purpose of the Infinite must unfold. The Trinity of Materialization consequently changes the way life is shaped within materialization. And in this way man's insights have changed all that is.

But because we are representative of the whole, the divine blueprints of the large picture can also be found underlying all situations of our life from the most mundane to the seemingly chaotic. Conflict resolution is no different; it mirrors the evolving of awareness through the four trinities of all that is. It moves from conflict to evolved awareness through the same four distinct stages displayed in the large picture.

The Four Stages of Conflict Resolution
Stage 1

In the Primary Trinity, the I AM gathers all that is uploaded to it from the insights of our lives, all new information about the mystery of beingness. But within the Infinite the same poles attract and within Creation opposite poles attract. The Primary Trinity, therefore, attracts all that resonates the same. In other words, it keeps and grows more luminous from that which it recognizes to be the same, namely that which is life-enhancing. The rest is passed on to the Creative Trinity for resolution.

In the first stage of resolution, we find our common ground. Unless this is first identified we cannot properly determine which parts to resolve in Stage 2. Failure to determine what we have in common with the opposition robs us of the priceless gift of becoming more knowledgeable by learning new aspects and view-points of that which we are (common ground). Too often, opponents prematurely focus on the differences during this first stage instead of simply assimilating the commonalities so that these initial gifts of insight can be received.

Stage 2

The Creative Trinity, having received all parts the I AM did not recognize as resonating similarly, now engages in analysis, weighing the unknown pieces against all that has been previously known. Once again it gathers to itself all that can be found to be the same (life-enhancing), examines it in a larger context and isolates that which is different. It now tackles the solving of these unknown pieces through externalizing them through Creation.

In this stage of conflict resolution a closer scrutiny of what is the same and what is different must take place. Those unknown pieces must be examined in depth, rather than taken at face value to extract common elements. It is necessary to examine these details in the context of the larger picture. Although we may have superficial differences, are we exploring a similar pattern? Are the core issues the same even though our method of dealing with them might be different? In this way the true differences to resolve are isolated from the similarities.

The last step is to creatively externalize them. Design a case scenario–objectively examine the issues as though they are happening to someone else. Reverse roles, honestly examining what it would be like to be in the other person's shoes.

Stage 3

Within the Trinity of Indwelling Life, opposites attract. The known (light) no longer pushes the unknown away, but instead desires to incorporate it within. It wants to turn the unknown into the known through experience. For this it needs form and so must create materialization.

In conflict resolution this stage requires that we abandon our preoccupation with our own viewpoint and genuinely try to understand the opposing position. The need now arises to create a situation to test the validity of the opposing viewpoint; to see and understand it better by observing it in action. Where the stakes are high, the testing of the unknown can be done in multiple, smaller controlled settings.

Your teenager wants to date. You feel she's too young, she feels you're ruining her life because all her friends date. After completing the previous steps, one or two controlled situations could be tested wherein she is dropped off and picked up by you and has to call you if she changes locations. This option is opposed to one requiring an absolute yes or no with one party or the other feeling unheard. An informed conclusion can then be drawn as to what can be supported.

Stage 4

In the Trinity of Materialization the unknown is incorporated into the known through experience. The previously unknown parts of the Infinite's being become known through our experiencing them and taking the time to gain the insights those experiences yield. New knowledge is gained.

In this stage we agree to disagree. The level of interaction is determined by what can be assimilated without being destructive to inner life or without being light and growth repressive. The key element of the success of this stage is to keep supporting the areas of common ground and the growth of all. Examples of the different degrees of interaction that could be allowed are:

• The in-laws don't like you, but they love your wife. Because they show their dislike when around you, you needn't be in their presence often but nevertheless support your spouse being with them as she chooses. If their intent is destructive, such as to break up the marriage, this needs to be clearly identified and the interaction must then be very minimal or terminated depending on the accompanying level of risk;

• If differences are only superficial but the common goals and philosophies are strong, we find we can live closely together or work together while honoring and supporting our diversity within our unity.

As we have moved through these stages, we have encountered the following ways of relating to each other:

• **Uniformity**–this is the stage of dependence on sameness to understand ourselves more fully;

• Exploring sameness vs. difference–co-dependence is experienced as we find sameness in the differences. We understand ourselves by observing that which we are not;

• **Exploring differences**–we seek our independence by focusing on that which we are not as mirrored by the other party. We determine whether the relationship is worth proceeding with;

• **Unity within diversity**–this is the stage of inter-dependence where we cooperate for the good of the common goals, supporting the diversity each contributes.

This final stage is the goal of all life since it provides the greatest opportunity for growth, whereas uniformity slows growth through stagnation. The more differences there are, the more uncomfortable the relationship will be; the greater the commitment to the greater goal, the more stable.

The Role of Anger

The cosmos expands outwards and contracts inwards like a huge doughnut rolling upon itself. For the cosmos to move over the edge on its journey back to the heart of God—back to the one-ness from which we sprang—anger needs to be brought into its proper place.

For emotion that is unresolved to be brought into resolution, increased perception is needed. The level of perception determines the emotion and in the same way, emotion also affects perception.

Everything in the cosmos, including anger, serves a purpose when viewed in the grand scheme of Creation. Its purpose is to break up stagnation or stuck patterns. The part of Creation most reluctant to yield to a higher order is what we call the dark—the portions of the Infinite's being that are as yet unknown.

Rage is the result of suppressed light. Thus when Lucifer and his hosts volunteered to embody the chaos and the unknown, they had to suppress their light, causing great rage to form. This rage can be utilized to break up the density so that those representing the light can turn the unknown into the known through experiencing it.

In the same way, our anger is the result of the portions of our lives that haven't yet yielded insights. It is the method our higher selves use to break up the stuck portions either within us or within our interaction with others. It is essential that we delve into our lives to find the origins of our anger and release those portions it signals as being stuck. In that way it relinquishes its hold over us. Failure to use anger for what it was really intended may cause events to trigger a flare-up that could injure or alienate the ones we love.

When our anger is the result of physical pain or great fatigue, it arises in a desperate attempt to try to change the situation. Unfortunately, it frequently ends up blindly lashing out at those in our environment because we can no longer see clearly and our rage becomes indiscriminate. At that point we cannot hear clearly either, because the improper use of anger causes tumultuous internal thoughts. We then end up attacking where it is a waste of energy, much like Don Quixote fighting windmills.

Anger can also surface as a result of ruts in our relationships. When it serves in this capacity, it will feel like the same old drama playing over and over and even though we have been patiently dealing with it until now, suddenly it reaches a peak and we find enough is enough. If this occurs, step out of the anger as it surfaces, recognizing its part in the bigger picture and allow it to express, but from this objective point of view. It is crucial, however, to direct it at the situation and not the person, so that it doesn't damage others and warp the interconnectedness of life, causing karma.

As light promoters, we need to cultivate enough discipline to stand back and determine whether expressing anger serves our purpose, which is to extract wisdom from experience. If it doesn't, we should find a harmless place to vent. Perhaps we are blessed with an understanding friend who will simply listen if we ask: "May I vent?" However, for the friend to try to 'fix it' is futile since we cannot hear properly at that point—only a listening ear is needed.

Whether our anger originates from the need to break up stagnant energy or from the frustration of life's burdens that makes us afraid we cannot bear them, we must become aware of its origin. Every reaction needs to be turned into a constructive response through perception. Energy is necessary for consciousness, so we need to be frugal and not drain it through wasted emotions. Furthermore, there is an enormous amount of energy tied up in old patterns that no longer serve us. By breaking up the old stuck areas, anger helps to release that energy for our use.

Any person or situation that still brings up painful or angry emotions or a knee-jerk reaction, should be carefully examined. Trace it back to the first occurrence where a similar event caused a similar response. Then extract from the experience the core insights by asking nine questions.

(Note that the first five questions assist us in seeing what is really going on. Use the intellect for this part because it was designed to help us discern what is behind surface appearances.)

1. **What is the lesson?** Look for the lesson that our higher self wishes us to embrace. For example, the lesson may be that we need to speak our truth. It could manifest as laryngitis, or someone may appear to mirror to us that we frequently suppress our voice. He or she may violate our boundaries to get our attention. We need to protect ourselves by voicing our truth that this behavior is unacceptable. Accepting the unacceptable isn't saintly, it is dysfunctional.

2. **What is the contract?** Everyone who interacts with us has made an agreement prior to this incarnation to assist with our growth and for us to assist in theirs. They may have agreed to push us over the edge, and we may do likewise for them. Ask, "What is the contract we are playing out?" It is with great love that many agreed while in the spirit world to be our catalysts. When we are in perfect equilibrium, there is no growth so it is a signal to the universe to knock us off balance so the lessons may continue. Thus we pull relationships into our lives that test us in every way imaginable.

3. **What is the role?** Am I playing the victim? Am I playing the teacher or the student? What role am I playing within this con-

tract? Also look at the role the other person is playing. For example, we may have a tyrant in our life. It may be our spouse, mother, or boss. Once you establish that, see who you are in relation to that person's role. Remember, we may change our role at any time because we create our reality.

4. **What is the mirror?** We pull relationships into our life that mirror one of the following things: an aspect of who we are, what we have given away, what we still place judgment on, or what we haven't developed yet. For example, if our innocence is gone, we may find ourselves intensely attracted to a young person. If we have given our integrity away, we might fall in love with a missionary who, in our eyes, represents integrity. Another thing that can be mirrored is that which we judge. If we have problems dealing with people who lie, then we are judging them and therefore attract liars.

5. **What is the gift?** Every person we encounter has come to give us a gift and receive one as well. This applies even with the most casual acquaintance. Ask, "What gift am I supposed to give this person?" It may be something as simple as offering him the gift of unconditional love; or we may recognize something beautiful in him that nobody else has seen. We may genuinely listen to someone and for the first time in years, they feel heard and understood.

(Note–The last four questions deal with our attitudes surrounding the answers to the first five questions)

6. **Can I allow?** This is the point of discerning what has to be allowed, what has to be changed, and finding the courage to act. Imagine yourself as the water in a river. If a rock is in front of you, should you oppose it or flow around the rock? We have masterfully created every situation in our life, even the rock. Is this a test of flexibility and surrender? Or is this a battle for us

to fight? A battle is only worth fighting if the stakes are worth winning. If you have already learned the lesson, no need to re-fight this battle.

7. **Can I accept?** We cannot accept the painful things that happen to us unless we begin to see the perfection underlying the web of appearances. A common belief is that we were placed on the wheel of reincarnation, suffering lifetime after lifetime, until we have lived enough lives to become perfect. We have been creat-ed perfectly with the ability to be a creator. Thoughts combined with emotions create our environment. The heart is like a microphone, the stronger the emotions, the stronger the uni-verse's response to manifest our desires. But the universe does-n't discriminate; it will manifest whatever we think—positive or negative. It is important that we accept that we have co-cre-ated the situation, which removes any feelings of having things done 'to' us.

8. **Can I release?** To release is to let go of the energy surrounding the person or event. If we don't release, we keep it alive by feeding it energy through thoughts (sometimes subconsciously). Even if someone has violated us in some way, working through these steps to gain the larger insights behind the appearances, changes the focus to an eternal perspective. It reveals the per-fection underlying the appearances.

9. **Can I be grateful?** If we have gone through the previous eight steps and can feel true gratitude for the insights gained, it raises consciousness. Gratitude is a powerful attitude that can assist us to transfigure into a higher state of being. It changes stumbling blocks into stepping stones.

If we have completed the first eight steps and don't feel grati-tude, going through them again to gain even deeper insights will help.

It is time for a more comprehensive understanding by the light promoters of what we deem our 'undesirable' pieces, or emotions. Too many believe they fulfill their part by focusing only on light and love. But over-polarizing towards the light is as detrimental to the evolution of awareness as over-polarizing towards the dark. In both instances stagnation occurs and evolution of awareness is retarded.

It is part of the universal law of compensation that we strengthen that which we oppose. This applies not only to traits within ourselves, but similarly to traits in others. On the other hand, acknowledging the perfection underlying the appearances surrounding anger lessens its hold on us and provides increased perception. Through perception comes transfiguration until eventually rage reveals those parts of life worth keeping. The rage that does remain becomes a valuable tool to extract insights from experience.

Cords

Cords are the result of worldviews and personal labels that have not been recapitulated. If the average person could see how bound they are by these limitations imposed by social conditioning, they would understand the enslavement to which they have submitted. The warrior of light spends a lifetime tracking his or her motives, working at eliminating worldviews and removing these ties that bind. The warrior then emerges a free, self-determinative being dwelling within the silence of mind to receive guidance from his or her inner wisdom.

The cords formed as a result of these conditioned limiting viewpoints can be seen on advanced Kirlian photography and can be removed by the intent of a healer or by ourselves. But just like any disease they will re-manifest if the misperception is not corrected. The fields of the body are instantly remarkably susceptible to healing, but for permanent repair of these fields and the often more gradual repair of the physical, the underlying misperception that caused the problem needs to be recapitulated.

Being a Peacemaker

Light-promoters frequently make the mistake of seeing physical concerns through rose-colored glasses of a spiritual vantage point and then treating them as though they are in fact spiritual rather than physical. Some examples of this would be:

• Bill loves his brother Sam, but his childhood experiences have made him inclined to find security in wealth. Through conniving manipulation, Bill cheats Sam out of his share of their inheritance. Because Sam can see how Bill has suffered and how much money means to him; because he also knows that deep down Bill loves him, he lets him get away with it.

  Conclusion: Sam believes himself to be acting magnanimously, but in fact he is injuring Bill. Bill can now keep his blindness in calling theft cleverness and has been allowed to create karma that will call similar circumstances forth on his own head. If he doesn't see clearly when he reaps his karma, it will have to happen again and again. Sam has foregone the opportunity to lovingly and firmly let Bill know that his conduct is unfair and unacceptable.

• Mary's eldest daughter seems to be floundering in every area of her life and Mary feels guilt because she believes she is partly responsible for not having been a better parent during a time when she was floundering herself. She keeps saving her daughter and finds that she has to do without in order to manage her budget as a result.

Conclusion: Seeing the reason for someone's shortcomings doesn't excuse them. We may have compassionate understanding for the cause of their behavior, but to indulge the behavior itself, keeps them locked into that position. Compensating for the lack in someone else's perception robs them of the opportunity to grow. When we keep someone from growing just to ease our guilt, we are acting selfishly.

If we serve the growth of all concerned, we will not view our role as peacemaker as one of covering someone's folly. To promote peace means to enhance growth as effortlessly as possible and sometimes it means to expose someone's flawed viewpoint. It would also mean helping someone ask the type of questions that can set them free from the treadmill of lack of perception. An example of this could be:

- There are three friends Jane, Sue, and Beth. Sue and Beth get into a disagreement and are trying to solve it through letters to each other. Sue sends all letters first to Jane to 'check over', asking whether it is sounding too adversarial and posing various other questions that skirt the main issue, namely that she is breaching a verbal agreement upon which Beth has relied and acted on for many months. Jane loves both her friends and wants to make peace. She therefore focuses on helping Sue write as nicely as possible, attempting to answer the irrelevant questions that divert focus from what is really going on.

  Even though she scrupulously tries to avoid giving advice, not pointing out that the questions don't really lead to the discovery of the core disagreement or problem, but actually prolongs it. As Sue asks more and more friends to advise her, and all give a neutral response or a response positive to her position (not knowing both viewpoints), she becomes further and further deviated from asking the core question: "Did I have a verbal agreement my friend depended on and am I going back on my word?" The mirrors around her have given no hint of any flaws in her reasoning and she is therefore becoming more convinced by the moment that her actions are justified.

If on the other hand, Jane realizes that by playing this avoidance game with Sue, she is not being a friend to either Sue or Beth, she may ask instead: "Where is the area of blindness in this matter?" She may then, after gathering facts from both sides, find the core of the disagreement. When this is pointed out with love, to one friend or another, the disagreement at least has a chance to be healed sooner rather than later.

In an attempt to avoid taking sides, or in a misguided effort to focus on the positive (which helps only if one is also prepared to point out the flaws in perception), peacemakers tend to complicate things. Every challenge has a core mystery or blind spot. No matter how much clearing of emotions has to be done, it must be accomplished for all involved to grow.

As peacemakers our task is to reveal the root of the conflict; to serve only indwelling life rather than the mirrors of illusion. Mirrors entrap–the truth sets us free.

CHAPTER FIVE

THE JOURNEY OF THE STARSEEDS

Flourishing vs. Surviving

The earth is emerging from a cycle of sleep. The time of its awakening, as the old cycle makes way for a new cycle of increased awareness, is only a few years away. Much has to de-structure within life as we know it, before this new period of light can be ushered in.

Humanity has already lost much of its vision, and therefore also much of its hope. The added burden of the seeming chaos of de-structuring could therefore be severely damaging. When the lower order makes way for a higher order, the loss of energy that results from the confusion could catapult humankind into an age of increased darkness rather than light.

It is for this reason that the way-showers have been sent–the ones who will be drawn to this book. They have come to be the torchbearers during the last years of darkness; to be a steady foundation of hope and vision when all that mankind has come to rely on fails. For the successful completion of their mission, they must learn to flourish rather than survive, by keeping their focus on the big picture even as the world around them crumbles.

These warriors of light have come to do battle against illusion, armed with the innocence of their hearts and the newness of their vision. They are strangers to the human experience, star–seeded among men. Many of these light-promoters find the cruelty and destructiveness of humankind crushing to their spirits. It is always confusing to encounter those qualities we do not possess ourselves.

If we allow confusion to drain the energy needed for consciousness, the hope of the world is lost. The hope and the solution rest upon us, the luminous ones who have come to show through the example of our own overcomings, that there is a way to flourish within adversity. By embracing our challenges as our greatest teachers, we can turn darkness to light, one step at a time.

Understanding the Insanity of Man

Seven planets were chosen to solve, within a loop of time, the failure of future events. Five have already self-destructed and the sixth, a 2nd dimensional civilization within the star system of Sirius will do so within the next twenty years.

If we do not successfully learn the lessons needed to redesign the future, the loop of time with all its painful experiences will have to be repeated again and again until we do. At this point, the last hope of success rests with the earth and humanity.

Humanity has lost its way, staggering like a drunk bearing a heavy burden up a steep mountain pass. The consequences of plunging to our destruction are unthinkable. Too many civilizations would plunge with us. Many star-seeds have come among us to bulwark and strengthen life on earth by their presence. They are here to gain insights from the folly of man, and in learning the lessons on their behalf, gently lift them off the treadmill of cycles of cataclysmic destruction.

For those of us who are here in service to mankind, the seeming insanity of the people of earth can be disheartening. If we allow ourselves to be overwhelmed by questions of why others act the way they do, we lose energy. In losing energy, we lose consciousness and run the risk of sinking into illusion ourselves. In order to fulfill our destiny as the ones holding the vision for humanity, we have to gain understanding of the problem and some of the pressures aggravating the problem, particularly as we find ourselves nearing the end of the loop in time.

The term 'insanity' refers to the condition of believing the unreal to be real. It is characterized by irrational emotions and conduct and the inability to see relationships between cause and effect. It takes very little insight to see that the definition as given applies to the conduct of man. Most believe the mirrors of material life to be real and because they have engaged in lifetimes of superficial lives, unprocessed emotions cause them to irrationally re-act rather than masterfully respond to life's challenges.

Not being able to foresee that by destroying their planetary habitat they are ultimately threatening the survival of the race, is a clear indication that humanity cannot see the relationship between cause and effect.

Twelve Reasons Why Man's Thinking Is Distorted:

1. The increased radiation experienced due to the holes in the ozone layer causes the same distorted thinking suffered by the

ancient Atlanteans. Just prior to the sinking of Atlantis, 9,564 years before the crucifixion of Christ, their disregard for the preservation of the environment caused a similar problem to occur.

2. As we have mentioned, the dark is becoming less dark, due to our turning it into the known (light) through experience. The light on the other hand, is becoming less light, as those of us who represent it take upon us some of the distortion of Lucifer and his hosts as a means of descending into this density. We then attempt to turn it into light through pulling in the experience necessary to gain its insights.

   As the polarity between light and dark decreases, the movement of the unfolding of the cosmos slows down: one year could become ten years. To us it would still seem like one year, but with ten years' worth of experiences crammed into it. The subjective feeling of this phenomenon is that time has accelerated.

   The stress of this accelerated experience of life has put an overwhelming strain on mankind. There is less time between challenges to gain the insights, and un-yielded insights pull in forced change (pain).

3. Because of the pain and stress, we are now in our third generation of drug users. Addictions are exponentially increasing as children see their parents use these coping mechanisms and they are becoming easier to obtain. Regular drug and alcohol use produces psychological distortions and as with any shelter in life, also creates stagnation.

4. Not only are there increased challenges, but because many cycles are coming to an end, karmic issues are coming up for resolution. Issues we have not solved for many lifetimes are painfully intense and carry unpleasant associations that are hard to pinpoint. This adds to the stress we are currently experiencing.

5. Ancient prophecies and scriptures have indicated that at this time, humankind would experience an unprecedented event:the chance to live for a period of about 20 years with two grids guiding our reality. A grid belonging to a species tells that species how to function. It is a geometric array of lines of light surrounding the earth.

   Since 1987 humanity has had not only the usual 3rd dimensional grid, but also a new 4th dimensional group consciousness grid; a love-based grid. At times, when we are not subject to fear, we manage to fleetingly access the higher consciousness grid, before crashing back to the fear-based grid. The result is a feeling of instability—of living in a type of spiritual 'manic depressiveness'.

6. There are technological methods in use by various unscrupulous groups intent on controlling the masses to sway the emotions of segments of the population in some geological areas.

7. There are alien interferences attempting to keep the consciousness of man from rising by programming rage and fear into the population. There are many races who have noticed that their future's beneficial outcome depends on our survival. Others have seen that every time we rise in consciousness, they seem to be pulled closer to what appears to them as extinction, but is in fact a rise into a higher overtone or dimension.

8. The multitude of waves from satellites, cell phones, radio, T.V. towers, and so forth, distort the informational relay between a species and its specific grid. Half of the species of songbirds have disappeared in the United States alone. Whales are beaching in increased numbers. Animals are exhibiting strange behaviors and migratory patterns. The same distortion can understandably be found among humans.

9. Solar flares are increasing in frequency. The energy fluctuations they cause could for moments weaken, or completely nullify the earth's electro-magnetic fields. Electro-magnetic fields hold memory in place. They also hold the gap between cause and effect. When we lose these fields even for a moment, it flushes up our unresolved pieces and forces us into chaotic change.

10. As computer learning replaces hands-on experiential learning, gaps in cognitive skills ensue. The abilities to think 'out of the box', and to mentally visualize abstract relationships are some of the abilities that suffer. It makes us less and less able to maturely connect the dots in areas of life beyond a specific expertise. In other words, our thinking becomes more and more two-dimensional.

11. Skipped emotional stages also impair thinking and increase irrational responses to life. If the family is disrupted and dysfunctional as a result of trauma, it takes seven generations to overcome the imbalance. Because of the 'speeding up' of events during specifically the last 2,000 years, traumas have been coming more frequently; two world wars and a depression have occurred for example in the last century. These global events overshadow the myriad of familial traumas that are no less devastating. When families don't have the time to heal and are overburdened by stress, childhoods are disrupted. Skills to enable each subsequent generation to build on the knowledge of the previous one are not taught. More refined skills, like how to grieve or find happiness, are overlooked in favor of learning how to survive. The emotional stages of childhood that are skipped create irrationality and impair judgment if not corrected through inner work.

12. Humanity in general has not been trained in the tools of discernment and in original thinking. They rely on external pro-

gramming to tell them how to be and what to do. They are therefore at the mercy of the unrealistic views of life portrayed by television, movies, and other media. The guidance of and trust in authorities have been eroded as media expose their flaws. As a result mankind is floundering and disoriented, not knowing where to look for its cues.

Unless one can see the bigger picture with its higher order however, the smaller picture can seem very chaotic. From the human perspective, the perfection of the overall plan becomes obscured because of the limited vantage point. We are the way-showers and have come as the solution to this earthly dilemma. We are the hope of the future and as such, have been blessed with the ability to make a huge difference.

If we deny the right of any part of creation to exist and fail to acknowledge that, even though we may not be able to see it, the folly and distorted perception of humankind has great value, we strengthen the madness. Before the inclusive gaze of a master able to see above the storm, illusion dissipates and reveals its lessons to the many eyes watching this final act of this great earthly stage play.

How to Protect Ourselves Against the Folly of Others

The belief is harbored by many that when we protect ourselves against the folly of others, we are strengthening it. It is somehow perceived as having faith in negativity and therefore in part causing it. Lightworkers are, as a result, often very unpleasantly surprised when their naive notions are battered by the unscrupulous behavior of their fellow man.

In assessing how much preparation against possible calamities we have to do, we have to ask how much we are prepared to lose. The first consideration concerns the most precious and sought after commodity in the cosmos: energy. Energy is required for the evolution of awareness. Shock or surprise drains energy and therefore lowers our awareness. The safeguarding of dearly earned levels of awareness is one of the most compelling reasons for being prepared.

The level of perception another is capable of is unknown and must be assessed through non-cognitive tools (feelings or symbols arising from meditation or dreams). Yet it is one of the most common causes of unpleasant surprises because we use the tools for assessing the known (reason) to judge another's level of consciousness. We may therefore think that a verbal agreement rather than a contract may be sufficient since the other person is so 'evolved'. Some considerations in this regard are:

- The more enlightened are often the ones who can see that the appearances of life are not real. If they are not yet able to access indwelling life, all they may clearly know is that they don't know. This leaves them vulnerable to outside influences that can sway or mislead them;
- Even someone in God-consciousness may be deluded by the self-assured opinions of another. Their minds are emptied of all social conditioning and until they access original thought in the Ascended Master stage they can yet be programmed by outside opinions
1. It is respectful to put an agreement in writing. It indicates that we take it seriously and value clarity. If the other person balks at it, they could have ill intent even at the beginning of the relationship.

We often ignore warning signs that something is amiss because we look at the 4th dimensional rather than the 3rd dimensional reality: "This person is mirroring my issues to me," may be accurate, but their conduct may still be unacceptable.

When we realize that most people do not engage in original thinking but react to outside influences, we can see how unstable and unreliable the majority must be. In matters of importance it is best to have a backup plan. If someone is supposed to pick up our child from kindergarten, for example, it is wise to leave an emergency pickup person's phone number with the teacher.

It is not possible for anyone to truly understand the complexities that make someone what he is; a unique perspective superimposed over all that is. Yet most seem to constantly seek understanding from another. Perhaps it is that people have so abandoned themselves that they seek identity in the mirrors around them. To further this futile attempt, they divulge their deepest secrets, assuming this to be intimacy.

Most relationships are based on the co-dependent triangle of conduct:

1. I give you whatever you want from me;
2. Because I give so much, I get to control you;
3. If you don't let me control you, I turn on you.

The very dear 'friend' can therefore as easily become tomorrow's enemy, armed with the secrets we so readily shared. If on the other hand, we truly see another instead of trying to be seen, we are engaging in genuine intimacy.

To overlook another's flaws does not strengthen relationship. If someone cannot manage money and we allow them to run us deeply into debt, we are bound to feel less loving and joyous about them than if we had taken their inabilities into consideration and curbed their spending. To see another's folly and prepare or protect ourselves against it, allows us the luxury of expecting the best. Having bolstered the weak areas of the relationship with damage control, we can allow ourselves to enjoy and accept the other person.

The Purpose of Action

"Until one is committed, there is hesitancy, the chance to draw back, always ineffectiveness concerning all acts of initiative and creation. There is one elementary truth, the ignorance of which kills countless ideas and splendid plan,s that the moment one definitely commits oneself, that Providence moves too. All sorts of things occur to help one that would never otherwise have occurred. A whole stream of events issues from the decision raising in one's favor all manner of unforeseen events, meetings and material assistance which no one could have dreamed would have come their way. Whatever you can do or dream, you can begin it. Boldness has genius, power and magic in it. Begin it now!"

Johann Wolfgang von Goethe, 19th Century German poet

The future, our destiny, outcome, all these are the unknown. When we have no familiarity with the tools used to access the unknown (refer to section on Tools of Discernment), feeling and dreaming, we tend to delay action until our reason tells us it is safe. Reason demands certainty of outcome even when it cannot be calculated. This want of predictability keeps the average person from realizing their full potential as they continually procrastinate until reason feels it can control the outcome.

The inability to determine when to act is further compounded by the average person's inability to read the mileposts that point us in the right direction–the signs in our environment. Much of the selfish and self-centered behavior of humans arises from the illusion that we have to fend for ourselves. It seems as though we are abandoned in the maze of life without a guidebook, lost and alone.

But all of life is interconnected; what damages one, damages all. Thus for those with eyes to see, all of life around us becomes our mirror, guiding each step we take. It is imperative to develop a communication system through which we can receive guidance from our sub-conscious and the web of life, the sub-conscious receiving it from our higher self.

For example, in the system of symbols I use to interpret my guiding signs, a car is the vehicle or mode of going through life. A crow means the path of power and food means spiritual nourishment. When I asked whether I should train individual students for the duration of their path to freedom from mortal boundaries, the following occurred: I drove my car to the store and as I tried to pull into a parking space, a crow sat eating an apple in the middle of that space. I inched closer and closer, but he just kept eating his apple. Finally I had to park right over him.

Because of the unusual behavior of the crow, I knew it was a sign. The way I was intending to move forward through life (the vehicle I had chosen, i.e., to start training apprentices) had arrived over the path of power which has to do with giving spiritual nourishment.

To me, a cat signifies temporal affairs. In trying to re-enter my driveway I saw a black cat run in two divergent directions. It did not seem possible and the way it was running was unusual. I almost missed the driveway. This warned me to not lose my way by allowing diverging, unresolved (black) temporal issues or things to pull me off course by diverting my attention.

Animals in normal behavior are not regarded as signs unless they stand out on the horizon of perception. The only time normal behavior should be interpreted as a sign is when it draws one's attention in a pronounced way.

For example, a car being driven down the street is not abnormal. But once, after having mentally posed a question to the universe about whether I had chosen the correct course of action involving a decision in my life, I noticed only white cars on the streets. This continued for at least ten minutes even though the individual cars were different. That told me to be at peace (white) with the way I had chosen to move forward.

In dreams every symbol is interpreted. A clear question asked before bedtime will generate an answer in the form of a symbol. A tape-recorder or notepad and pencil will help record this information. Dream signs even answer questions we didn't ask, illuminating the blind spots that obscure our vision and impede our progress.

At times when choices and signs seem obscure and we feel we are floundering, action can break the stalemate. Action can serve the purpose of showing us which direction we should not take so we can identify the right course. Action can be better than doing nothing and with pure intent we may find our destiny.

When our actions are in a rut, lifeforce closes down and pain will enter our life to signal that change is needed. To continually take actions that expose us to new opportunities, on the other hand, pulls in new lifeforce. This is because it puts us in the fast current of the river of life where life is ever fresh and our chances of serving the Infinite through learning from experience are maximized.

We knock on every door before us so that we can see which ones open. But seeking opportunities to learn through experience does not mean we scatter our energies unnecessarily. As sovereign beings we do not waste energy through actions that are attempts to please others. We stand in stillness and power in the middle of our circle, responding only to the instructions of our higher self as received through the guidance of our hearts. In this way we render the highest service to all life.

Our actions are done without attachment to outcome. When we are able to hear the promptings from within and read the signs without, we have become fully cooperative with the unfolding of life; we have become a clear channel for the light of God.

The Value of Taking Risks

Shakespeare's characters were sometimes real people and sometimes the personification of personality traits. He had the ability to give a characteristic a name and a voice that was unsurpassed. He said: "I your looking glass shall be and reveal to you things that you yourself know not of".

Shakespeare's Julius Caesar can be called the personification of courage. He said of fear: "We are two lions littered in a day, and I the elder and more terrible. And Caesar shall go forth." Like all great men, he knew that fear can paralyze and immobilize anyone who would indulge and entertain its presence. He said: "Of all the wonders that I yet have heard, it seems to me most strange that men should fear, seeing that death, a necessary end, will come when it will come." Anyone with this kind of attitude and the courage to back it up must succeed in life.

Julius Caesar was an epileptic, a condition many would use as an excuse not to succeed. He built a good, useful and robust courage by doing things that were hard to do. He swam the Tiber river everyday when in Rome while others watched from the bank. He took risks when others stood back.

In Shakespeare's play, Cassius and the other Roman leaders thought they saw Caesar's ghost after his assassination. Even after his death he remained a force to be reckoned with. One by one they started to commit suicide, driven by their fears and their doubts.

In some way, all failure is suicidal because we bring it about ourselves. The only true failure is failure to learn. As we steadfastly keep the larger purpose of life in mind, namely the evolution of awareness through the exploring of the mysteries of beingness, we become unattached to outcome. Each battle is a battle for perception–we have nothing to prove and everything to learn.

For a life of adventure and risk–a life in which we can make the greatest contribution to the One expressing as the many–we have come to the right place. It is here in this density, where the stakes are high and all new knowledge is gained. The diligence with which we tackle this role as explorers of consciousness depends on our willingness to take risks and to extend the boundaries of our comfort zones.

Many seek the comfort of the familiar and the safety of the known, over-polarizing towards the light. The irony of the situation is that the safety of the known is anything but safe: life is set up to prod stagnation with forced change, which is pain. That which is used to break up the shelter of stagnation and force us into change, is anger or rage.

Anything that helps us avoid actively participating in the experiences of life and keeps us from growing through increased perception, attracts rage from outside sources. The passive always attracts the proactive. Any escape from our own negative emotions manifests them in outside circumstances and strengthens them within. We are then either faced with having to increase the avoidance or experience increased emotional outbursts.

Some shelters or ways to avoid having to confront life include drugs, alcohol, work, living vicariously through TV or books and using meditation as an escape into bliss rather than a non-cognitive information gathering technique. Some of these shelters are certainly valid ways to relax, but can become a substitute for vibrant living if used excessively.

The destiny of man is to push the existing limits of what is known; to take risks through developing a strong, useful courage. Within this density, the value of pushing beyond our comfort zones has become obscured. We are taught to think things through and not to take unnecessary chances. But to be valiant in exploring the unknown through experience, we have to go beyond where logic or reason can predict the outcome.

That which we have undertaken to solve on behalf of the Infinite has never been solved before during all previous cycles of life. As always when dealing with the unknown, the feelings of our hearts will show the way, even when reason argues otherwise. It will require passion and trust in the perfection of the greater purpose—much like the ancient mariners that launched their ships on an unpredictable voyage and into uncharted seas. There is no certainty of outcome, only the deep conviction that to plunge forward, with all our hearts is infinitely better than to disengage from life by staying in the safety of the harbor until storms forcefully cast us adrift.

Predictability Makes Us Vulnerable

The river of life, or the flow of awareness, moves inexorably forward creating change. This ever-changing flow of life exploring itself is the one constant we can count on. Just as the water and motion of the river are never the same from moment to moment, so too life breaks down any attempt to hold on to the old.

Old patterns we tend to hold on to include: old coping mechanisms; events that have not yielded their insights but still pull our triggers; old identities we give ourselves; flaws we have not converted to wisdom and many other old habits and ruts we have created for ourselves.

These patterns we carry through life make us predictable and therefore vulnerable. Anyone who gets to know and observe these predictable patterns within us can use them against us. Today's marriage may turn into tomorrow's divorce; the business relationship that started out so amicably may turn into the most hostile lawsuit. In fact, because life doesn't want us to keep holding on to these stuck patterns, it will encourage us to see that they do not serve us by producing such adversarial circumstances. So predictability leaves us vulnerable and exposed from all angles.

Let us examine some of these areas that allow life, through our relationships, to stalk us.

- **Past events** that have not yielded insights and therefore still pull our triggers can easily be used to manipulate us. For example: Frank has had sexual abuse by a member of the same sex and therefore has an almost phobic reaction when there is homosexual interest directed at him. If a competitor at work discovers this, he can let it be known that Frank is the target for his boss's sexual interest. Even though Frank may try to hide his resulting phobic reaction, he may immediately try not to be in the same room with his boss, not make eye contact or avoid attending meetings because he feels everyone suspects he's having a sexual relationship with his boss. The boss may think Frank is losing interest in his work and pass him by when it's time for promotions.

- Revealing our identity to another is equally dangerous. Joe says to his wife that the only way he will physically slap a woman is when she needs to be brought out of a hysterical condition. She then begins to have an affair and wants him to be removed from the house. She pretends to be hysterical and when he slaps her, she calls the police. She accuses him of threatening her safety, and Joe is given a restraining order that keeps him away from her and the house.

- When we have a need, another can use it as a hook. This dynamic has been mastered by the co-dependent people of the world. The game is played over and over again until the co-dependents get quite proficient at gauging the other person's need, offering to meet it in exchange for what they want. In this way, most relationships are determined not by our highest wisdom, but by our most prevalent needs.

• Being in a rut makes us easy to stalk. Many victims of rapes, murders, or robberies were carefully studied by their attackers who used their predictability against them.

Our life should not be lived expecting the worst. But in order to have the luxury of expecting the best we have to be prepared for the worst. We will be taken by surprise if we leave ourselves vulnerable, draining the energy for awareness. Although the examples given are about leaving ourselves vulnerable to manipulation from others, the real adversary is life itself. The purpose of the Infinite to evolve awareness through material life does not allow stuck, predictable portions of existence to stay that way for long.

To maximize learning about the mysteries of the Infinite's being at this level, as much diversity as possible is needed. Where uniformity or old patterns of behavior exist, life-force is diminished. Where life's experiences, and our approach to tackling the challenges life brings, are constantly new and evolving, life-force increases.

We find ourselves in the position of either cultivating the awareness of what no longer serves our highest level of perception and letting it go, or life will do it for us. Some criteria in determining what has become obsolete are:

• Does this choice reflect my highest identity as a being as vast as the cosmos having a human experience?

• Does this choice make my heart sing and reflect my highest perception?

- Does this situation give me a knee-jerk reaction? If so, there are unyielded insights around similar issues in life that I need to find, so that I no longer need to manifest situations like this.
- Do I feel expanded by a particular relationship or activity or do I feel contracted and drained or diminished?
- When approaching an unknown situation, am I falling into the traps of someone who has taken the illusions (mirrors) of life at face value by responding in one or more of the following ways?
  1. Thinking I know what's going on;
  2. Obsessing about the question, which drains energy;
  3. Only acknowledging what fits into already held belief systems and either attacking, ignoring, or ridiculing the rest.

Or instead, am I acknowledging that each person and situation and moment is new and unique and must be approached with the utmost awareness and open-mindedness?

The end–reward of eliminating the predictable from our lives is a fluidity of being found among those who have mastered themselves. When we fully co-operate with the changes that bring growth, our opposition to life is surrendered. No longer hiding in the perceived safety of our shelters, we embrace our challenges and rekindle the flame of our passion for life, pouring our hearts into every experience.

Becoming the Seven Directions

All things in the cosmos are by their nature aligned to one direction (one of the elements or building blocks of Creation) or another. The sub-personalities are no exception. Each direction is also represented by an element.

As we bring the inner nurturer, inner child, inner sage and inner warrior into balance and expression during the Adept phase 2 of ego-identification, the elements of earth, fire, water and air are also brought into balance. We become the four directions in that we embody their qualities, ancient and eternal.

In the second phase (bliss phase) of God-consciousness we balance the direction of below, having stepped into the middle of our circle at the time of disconnecting from ego. The element of below is love.

During the phase of bliss, the seer's love floods across all boundaries. For the heart to fully open, the mind must be still—which it is at this point. The love that pours forth is therefore beyond anything that can be experienced while the inner dialogue exists during identity consciousness.

The love is so all-encompassing that the seer is very vulnerable to exploitation. The element of love flooding the cells of the seer's body begins the process of preparing it for immortality during the next stage of Ascended Master.

During the second phase of the Ascended Master's stage, he or she must become one with the element of light so the cells can be filled with light and spiritualized to such an extent that they can become immortal or eternal matter and the master can become the I Am That I Am.

At the end of the Ascended Mastery stage, the direction of within comes into full expression, flooding the Ascended Master with the first building block of All That Is: Original Awareness, the primary element.

To bring Original Awareness into full embodiment, original thinking must become a part of life. Learning to fully surrender to it, however, is done throughout all three phases of Ascended Mastery. Having gotten rid of old conditioning, the master finds him or herself in a mental 'vacuum' either to be filled with outside cues yet again, or flooded by original thinking from Source itself.

When Original Awareness is fully accessed, the direction of within becomes one with the Ascended Master and he becomes the door of everything. To understand this deeply esoteric concept, imagine an X with the upper part going on and on forever and the lower part doing the same. The body is the crossing point.

All that is lies without and also within. There is no inside or outside and wherever the body is, is the center of all existence. When we truly internalize this perception, we begin to consciously affect all life. It is at this point that we enter the God-kingdom.

> *"List ye again, O Man, to my wisdom, that hearing*
> *ye too might live and be free. Not of the earth are ye–*
> *earthly but of the Infinite Cosmic Light."*
> Emerald Tables of Thoth, Tablet IV

Feeling at Home on Earth

As the out-breath and in-breath of God create the greatest expansion and contraction cycles within the macrocosm, so too are they mirrored within the microcosm. There are those who live primarily in expansion (output) and those who live in contraction (input). Feeling at home within life on earth requires first that we familiarize ourselves with these principles and then create balance between these expanding and contracting cycles in our lives. (See Figure 23, The Cycles of Expansion and Contraction)

Living Within Expansion

Those who live primarily in a state of expansion are the people with wings. They want to explore, to achieve, to conquer and to live a life full of adventure that pushes the boundaries of the known into the unknown. They are the fire-carriers who reach for the new and find ruts and routines soul-deadening. Their love is poured into what they do, which is passion.

The Cycles of Expansion and Contraction

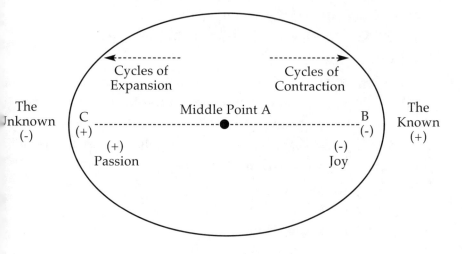

C=our own inner masculine (+)   B=our own inner feminine (-)

The degree of attraction is determined by how far apart the poles are in degrees. The further apart, the stronger the attraction. When the cycle of expansion goes all the way to C, it is further away from the negative pole of B than that of the unknown and snaps back into contraction.

(Figure 23)

227

Type of Energy

The electrical (masculine) energy is dominant over the magnetic (feminine) energy and as a consequence these individuals sometimes prefer the fall and winter when the magnetic energy is stronger and helps balance their over-abundance of electrical energy. Their pursuits are active rather than passive. Their mental activity is very strong and they might find it difficult to relax.

Positive Tendencies

They like being a cause rather than an effect. They like to build and turn their goals into realities. Their strong suit is original thinking and problem solving. They delve into the unknown where growth originates and therefore grow and change rapidly. They prize achievement and growth.

Negative Tendencies

If growth is too rapid, their ambitions can be very ungrounded and lack the proper foundation. People lose their sovereignty when they have wings but no roots in that they feel the need for a place of grounding. They yearn for a home, and tend not to nurture themselves; this makes them susceptible to manipulation in relationships. In some instances, they become over-sexed in an attempt to bring their lower chakras into balance. They sometimes tend to be inattentive during relationships.

Causes of Over-Balance

Social conditioning that stresses that the value of the individual lies in what he does, rather than who he is, is a significant factor in causing this over-balance. It may also be the result of unresolved past events such as a very stressful home life, or issues that cause the need to prove himself. Another contributing factor could be a worldview resulting from past life experiences where passiveness produced calamity.

Solution

The higher the flight of an individual's thought, the greater the need for roots. The inner child and inner nurturer in expression provide a source of magnetic energy to help create wholeness within. A concerted effort needs to be made to incorporate nurturing elements into one's environment. For example: cozy shoes to wear under one's desk; packing a favorite pillow and blanket for a hotel stay; a back support and favorite music in the car and a stash of protein drinks or herbal teas available during regular breaks.

Nature experiences must be scheduled into this active achiever's life. Twenty minutes a day will help enormously, as well as a few hours each weekend. These experiences need to be passive – active sports is still concerned with doing rather than being. These should be times of input and receptiveness, rather than output.

Living Within Contraction

Those living within contraction have traditionally been priests and shepherds rather than kings and conquerors. They seek joy versus passion; to walk in a cool, green forest rather than search for a lost treasure. Their roots are deep and their connection with the earth strong. They enjoy simple pleasures and get contentment from creating.

Type of Energy

Their magnetic energy dominates their electric energy. They tend to value security and are therefore not fond of taking risks. They are the water bearers and value the quality of the journey over the end-results. They are receptive and their energy more passive.

Positive Tendencies

Those who are over-balanced in their magnetic energy tend to feel at home wherever they go. They are nurturing to self and others and generally are comfortable around others. If their basic needs are met, they find contentment in the experiences of everyday life. They excel at creating a pleasant atmosphere around offices and warmth within the home. They bring creativity and quality to the journey of life.

Negative Tendencies

Those living within contraction tend to over-polarize towards the light (the known) where they feel safe and secure. But because growth is found through embracing the unknown (the dark or un-yielded light), they tend to stagnate. They are less adept at original thought and planning and therefore lack confidence in their ability to achieve. This can cause a lack of sovereignty and a neediness that can be manipulated in relationships. When such a person feels very disempowered, they can become destructive and critical of those attempting to build and achieve. Some use meditation as an escape from challenge (television and other addictions can also be used as an escape). Others may become obsessive about self-nurturing.

Causes of Over-Balance

When past life and childhood experiences reveal the world as unsafe and unstable, the desire to remain in the safety of the known becomes obsessive. Risk taking and venturing into the unknown becomes undesirable. This type of over-balance also occurs when someone grows up in a household where the peace is disturbed by bouts of threatening rage. Passion is then seen as destructive.

Solution

To bring new energy in to dispel the stagnation, new experiences must be pulled into their lives. A deliberate attempt must be made to push the boundaries of their comfort zone a little bit further every day until their wings allow them to fly. Looking ahead and setting a goal, then breaking the goal into projects and the projects into daily tasks, will help build confidence and self-determination.

Whenever there are pieces within that are undeveloped, we become invested in finding them without, giving our power to another to complete us. But balance cannot be found without if it is not found within. This means the flow of awareness has to shatter that relationship in order to mirror to us that an outside source is not a reliable place to find our sustenance.

As long as we have wings without roots, we will be dependent on another to make us feel at home. Conversely, as long as we have roots without wings, we will stagnate and draw in pain to prod us into change and growth. We will also need to rely on others to help us achieve. When we become confident in our ability to determine our future, we balance the expansion and contraction cycles of our lives. We will cease to yearn for the higher spheres from whence we came but instead grow in feeling the satisfaction of being at home on earth.

The Laws of the Cycles

To understand why these cycles move in expansion and contraction, pulsing from one to the other, we have to remember that there are degrees of polarity. One thing can be a little negative in relation to another and a third thing can be very negative in relation to it.

As the door of everything, we have the same vastness within as we have without and the same laws apply. Therefore, the same principle will snap us back from expanding too far into passion for example, as it would in turning the outbreath of God to the inbreath. In human lives, someone who has somehow lost this safety mechanism that prevents cycles from going out of bounds becomes manic depressive.

As shown in Figure 21, the unknown has a negative polarity as has our own inner feminine, which holds our own unknown portions. The known has a positive polarity, as has our own inner masculine, which holds our own known pieces.

As we delve into the unknown of our world, desiring to know it (which is passion), we are traveling from A to C. The emotion of passion has a positive polarity and is drawn by the negative polarity of the unknown. On our circular graph (See Figure 23, The Cycles of Expansion/Contraction) the further poles are apart, the greater the degree of polarity and the stronger the attraction.

By the time the expansion has moved all the way to C, it is further away from its own feminine pole B, than the feminine unknown without and is therefore suddenly more attracted to its own inner negative pole. This therefore pulls the expansion back to the stronger attraction of B into contraction and the desire to live (joy).

By the time life is pulled all the way to B, the pull from C becomes so strong that it pulls everything into expansion again. The momentum of any cycle is fastest immediately after it reverses direction, slowing down the further it progresses. We can therefore expect that the first part of the blue road home will occur very rapidly.

The further we expand into the unknown, i.e., the further we extend A-C; the further we snap back and extend A-B, making our circle large and larger. As a practical matter it means that the more valiant we are in fulfilling our agreement to explore the unknown portions of existence, the deeper our joy becomes.

In exactly the same way, the other three sets of emotional poles pulse and help each other grow: Fear (-) shows us what parts of existence we have not yet included in our love (+). Anger (+) breaks up that which is no longer needed so we can see clearly what is worth protecting (-) or fighting for. Pain (+) as the desire to change, removes that which is not life-enhancing so we may find that which we desire to keep, which is contentment (-). In this way the dynamic balance of our emotional cycles stays intact even as the cycles become larger and larger and we include more and more of existence in our experience.

Finding Our Passion

When the social conditioning of our lives has left the clear impression that it is unsafe to fully participate in the game of life, we may hang back in the safety of the known, afraid to make ourselves a target by being noticed. We may fear that passion could cause our light to shine so brightly that others might try and tear us down so that their own lack of luster isn't as obvious.

If we deny our desire to express passionately long enough, we will end up being strangers to passion; not knowing how to find it nor recognize it even if we do. The lateral hypothalamus tells us when we have eaten enough. The ventromedial hypothalamus tells us when we are hungry. In the same way, if we deny the promptings from these portions of the brain, we will end up either obese or anorexic. When that happens we have to gently coach ourselves into recognizing what their promptings feel like.

When passion beckons we feel warm and excited, our faces flushed and our imagination stirring with questions of "What if?" and "What lies beyond the next horizon?" It inspires us into action and gives us the belief that we can take risks and build.

We find our passion by following the yearnings our moments of joy evoke within our hearts. It is the lost song the singer feels hiding within the shadows of his mind. It is the lost rhythm the dancer forever seeks. It is the mysteries of the cosmos that wait for the scientist or the metaphysician to unlock. It is the desire inspired by the innocence in our child's eyes to build a life of wonder and beauty for our family.

If passion has become a stranger to us, we might have to become acquainted with it one facet at a time. When expressed, passion consists of taking risks; of accomplishment and the building of something new. It adds new experiences, further boundaries, and new depth to our lives.

To train ourselves to hear the voice of passion once again, we find the yearning of our heart and follow where it leads. We make a concerted effort to break free from the prison bars of ruts and expectations, socially conditioned limitations and self-imposed belief systems that keep us in mediocrity. We take a few minutes a day to dare to dream of what would make our hearts sing. We awake each morning and determine to live the day before us as though it were our last. We look at our lives as though for the first time, with a fresh perspective that can detect the joyless, self-sacrificing areas. With courage and great consideration for the consequences of our actions on others, we implement our first steps to bring the glow of passion back to these areas.

A decision may take a minute to make, but for it to be as life-altering as we would want it to be, it needs to be supported by a firm foundation. This requires planning and also a certain amount of analysis. What is the goal? What resources will be needed? Is there a discrepancy between what we need and what we have and how can we fill it? Many businesses fail, taking many dreams with them, because not enough thought is given to what is needed to support them in terms of time and money. Once a goal is identified, break it into projects and tasks. Jack London is one of the highest paid authors if one takes inflation into consideration. He used the same method for achieving success. An immigrant and dockworker, Jack London had a dream of breaking free from the hard grueling labor and becoming an author. Before his long day began, he studied English grammar for an hour, and then worked to earn his bread and butter as a dockworker. At night, he took a creative writing class at the library and when he got home, he did his writing. His goal was broken up into projects, then into tasks and his day structured to accommodate them.

Many envy the achievements of others, but they are not prepared to put in the work. Sometimes it takes burning the candle on both ends to fulfill a dream. It is our passion that keeps our enthusiasm lit and gives us our second wind to fly higher than we ever thought possible.

Finding Our Joy

As passion explores the multitude of possibilities through which we can express, so joy is concentrated on the simplicity of the moment. Joy is a mindset, a certain focus that sees the perfection of the here and now, casting a golden glow over the experiences of yesterday. It turns the mundane into poetry and captures the moment in a still life image.

Milton said: *"The mind in its own place and of itself can turn hell into heaven and heaven into hell"*. The great English master painter, Turner, at the end of his life said that in his entire life he'd never seen anything ugly. Franz Lizt was urged to write his memoirs, but he said: *"It's enough to have lived such a life"*. He found such joy in his experiences, he didn't have to externalize them to appreciate them.

Joy can be recognized by the deep feeling of satisfaction it brings; by the feeling that one has come home to oneself. It taps into the quiet place within that nurtures the soul and replenishes the mind. When under its spell, joy makes us feel light and young again, connected to the earth and freed from our cares.

The key to finding our joy lies in our ability to work with time. In a world where mounting responsibilities urge us to accomplish more in less time, most tasks are hastily performed. Yet we don't seem to have any more time to enjoy life. The time that is supposed to be leisure time has even more undone chores competing for it. The reason this is so is that when we rush, we speed up time and we seem to have even less at our disposal.

Just as building with passion requires careful and disciplined time allocations, living with joy requires the ability to compress time. If we focus on the details in front of us at this moment, time slows down. Even if we cannot find an hour today to do the things we enjoy, we can find the time to enjoy the things we are doing. In cutting up vegetables to make a stew, we can see the colors of the carrots, explore the different textures of each vegetable, smell the fresh fragrance as we cut through their skin.

Even repetitive work can become a mantra, or a production line a prayer as we send blessings and angelic assistance to the homes where the products will end up. Walking in the crowded street, we can feel the sadness of others but can turn it into joy by envisioning blessings pouring into their lives. The loss in the lives of others can be used to inspire praise and gratitude for the blessings in our own.

In our choice of the joy to fill our leisure time, we look for that which will inspire us into achievement. As the joy flows inward on the surface, the passion it inspires folds outward beneath the surface. The greater our joy, the greater the actions it will inspire.

Letting Our Light Shine

Traditionally, it hasn't been safe to let our light shine; to demonstrate too great a passion or too deep a joy. It has brought about persecution from the tribe whose lack of luster becomes apparent by comparison. Tribes exist everywhere people see the safety of uniformity and these groups reject that which cannot be controlled.

When confronted with anything superlative that lies beyond the status quo, the tribe has the uncomfortable choice of either living with excellence in their midst and feeling less by comparison, changing their own behavior to match the new standard or, alternatively, to eject from the tribe the ones who excel.

Throughout history those who have demonstrated great passion or joy have been all too frequently ostracized and shunned. The great ones in our midst have found that more often than not, the price of greatness has been solitude. But to still our inner song to conform to mediocrity is psychological suicide. We have come too far through space and time to be the wayshowers of this planet, to allow ourselves to blend into the grayness of the unaware masses.

Surrounded by our own inner family, driven by passion and sustained by joy, let us with courage walk the path of a life well lived. Let us fulfill our destinies as light beacons unto the world.

Living a Balanced Life

There is a saying, "Life is a journey, not a camp". We are either moving forward or moving backwards, but we are never standing still. In the vast river of change we call life, any life form either moves with it, or is swept away to be replaced by another.

Lifeforms that consistently oppose life may, after many lifetimes, even lose the ability to incarnate into physicality at all. Lack of growth weakens the lifeforce at someone's disposal. Without sufficient lifeforce and energy, the formation of a lower or physical body cannot take place. It requires an enormous amount of energy to create material form.

Because everything is in constant flux, balance cannot be stationary–it has to consist of movement. Many light seekers think of balance as always living in serenity and peace no matter what occurs. What they fail to understand is that by refusing to embrace the dark, they call it forth. Anything that we deny the right to exist by failing to acknowledge its contribution within the cosmos, is strengthened either within us or within our environment.

We are the microcosm of the macrocosm, but the macrocosm is anything but peaceful and serene. Although some parts of it may be tranquil, it is also destructive and explosive and gloriously passionate. The only constant is the matrix; the underlying grand scheme that gives the overall purpose and the allotted time and space within which creational cycles play out.

As we enter God-consciousness, we see the big picture. Not until we re-enter the human condition do we pay attention to the stormy ups and downs of life. Even as we cry and laugh once more in the drama of human life, we still keep our inner focus on the big picture; the perfection of the divine plan. Like the cosmic matrix that underlies the passionate drama of the cosmos, this large inner perspective underlies the stormy changes in our lives. It provides stability within flow, measure within movement.

Keeping our eyes fixed on the perfection underlying appearances can be called the first half of balance. It is the masculine, positive polarity of balance. Learning to bring balance to the movement or flow of emotion is the second half of balance, the feminine, magnetic aspect. If we have expanded vision, without allowing the balanced interaction of emotion to occur, growth stops and we start to stagnate. When emotion is denied the right to exist, it eventually surfaces as jagged and disproportionate; in other words, out of balance.

Anger is often shunned, whereas joy is valued. Few utilize the immense value of anger and learn how to bring it into balance. To the same degree that it is suppressed, anger will surge and frequently become destructive. The more we identify anger with destructiveness, the more we tend to suppress it and in this way an escalating imbalance builds up that not only stifles anger, but also joy.

The great gift of anger is that it breaks up stuck patterns. If we allow anger to surface, not directing it at another, but simply feeling it throughout our being, it can run its course. When it is spent ask the question: "What can I now see that I couldn't see before?" If we question persistently enough, hidden insights will reveal themselves. Increased perception brings increased energy and power, which in turn increases our desire to live. The desire to live is joy. The desire to live in turn propels us into an exploration of life and the unknown. The unknown portions of life are the most 'stuck' of all parts of existence and have not yielded during all previous creational cycles. Anger is therefore needed to assist in breaking up the illusion.

In this way, opposite emotional forces within us yield each other. Fear alerts us to those parts of creation we have not yet included within our compassionate understanding so that our love can grow. Passion and joy alternate by prompting each other.

As all these inner components are given equal value, a dynamic, growth-promoting balance is born. A back and forth flow and movement provides the impetus to help drive us upward along the spiral of awareness. The steady gaze we keep on the large picture, on the other hand, provides the balance we need to ensure that we maintain an eternal perspective.

The Journey Back to the Heart of God

The Red Road

The out-breath of God, the cycle of expansion away from the heart of God, has been designed to explore the unknown. Driven by the emotion of passion, we have been journeying on the red road away from Source into realms made dense by unyielded light.

This universe, the densest and newest of all universes, has been on the cutting edge where all life pushes into the unknown. In these dense levels light and frequency are easily distorted. Here, the passion with which we, the One expressing as the many, set out on this journey of exploration, often becomes aggression. This is particularly the case when not balanced with joy.

From a very large perspective, our journey has slowed and progress has become more labored. The law of compensation decrees that when something is taken away, something else has to be given. Because of the loss of speed in our progress, diversity is substituted. Not only are our learning opportunities enhanced by the great diversity of life forms in this density, but also by the diversity of experiences.

The slowing down of the cosmic movement has slowed time. As a result, a given period such as a year may still feel like a year to us, but contains many more experiences to learn from since it may actually be the equivalent of ten years. Psychologically it feels as though time has sped up.

As previously mentioned, the first reason for this slowing of the cycle of expansion is that the polarity between dark and light has lessened. Second, on the edge of the cycle of expansion, we're starting to be pulled not only forwards by the unknown, but also backwards by our own inner feminine. When we reach the edge of time and space allotted for this cycle of expansion, the pull from our own feminine will finally prevail and pull us back on the blue road home.

The red road on the journey of expansion and the blue road on the journey of contraction can be compared to the red blood moving through the arteries away from the heart, and the blue blood moving back through the veins. We receive non-cognitive information from the various levels of light through the miniscule chakras located in every cell. This is then downloaded into the red arterial blood. As blue blood it returns to the heart where it is interpreted by the thymus.

The red road we have been on has been dominated by mental energy. It has ballooned into greater and greater complexity. Like the red blood, it has become laden with information to be carried with us back into oneness, that the One may become enriched by the experiences of the many.

As a microcosm of the macrocosm, life on Earth mirrors the state of increasing complexity: in its population explosion, its consumerism, its ballooning budget deficits and inflation, its inflated debt structures, the increasing complexity in judicial and governmental sections, the escalating burden on the environment. All these are indicators that the electrical (masculine, mental) is so overbalanced that we are ready to catapult into contraction.

The Blue Road

Whether we speak of the blue road, the cycle of contraction, of life on earth or in the cosmos, they will have many similarities. First, the change from expansion to contraction happens in the twinkling of an eye when critical mass is reached. Second, at the beginning of either cycle, when our journey is influenced by the very strong pull of only one opposite pole (unlike at the end of a cycle when our journey is pulled by two opposite poles like a tug of war), change is incredibly rapid.

The most dominant characteristic of our journey home is its destructuring nature and its tendency to simplify and reduce. Much of what we know will simply become obsolete. The criteria for what remains is whether it increases joy within the cosmos. To provide joy to all life, it has to be enhancing of indwelling life.

As the cycle of contraction is emotional and introspective, the best preparation light-promoters can make is to come home to themselves; to achieve a balanced relationship with their inner pieces and attain emotional sovereignty. It is essential that we gain the unshakeable realization that our being is our sustenance; that we become our own source of happiness and support. The mode of seeking what we need outside ourselves is prevalent during the time life expands, but will not survive the time of contraction.

We are entering a time when life will get rid of that which has not yielded its insights. It is time for the shallow life filled with unexamined diversity to make way for deep, meaningful living. If we shed those things in life that cannot make our hearts sing, they can be gracefully replaced by what does, or we can wait for cataclysmic change to do it for us.

The reason we have depleted not only our environment, but also ourselves, is because of our insatiable appetite to fill ourselves from the outside and since this cannot be done, we take far more than we need. Frugality does not mean that we forfeit abundance, but that we cease to need and therefore receive from a position of fullness only that which is ours to take.

As our inner world becomes our strength and support, we act only when needed. We fight only those battles where perception can be gained and we interact sparingly with others. No longer do we waste energy with words. Our life has become the disciplined life of a warrior against illusion. Like a master, we find our joy in the moment, gracefully surrendering to change–our hearts leading the way.

The Gifts of the Cycles of Life

The nature of the cycles of expansion is to build. The nature of the cycles of contraction, on the other hand, is to de-structure. When the cycles are out of balance the gifts of these cycles of life aren't delivered and their nature becomes distorted. For instance, de-structuring can become destructiveness and passion can become aggression.

Even when the cycles are in balance, if we are unaware of the gifts inherent in their nature, we cannot fully reap their benefits. The ones we call saints (s = snake, an = heaven, the ones who co-operate with the spirals of awareness), have always been those who have first gained the hidden insights of the cosmic forces and their rhythms, and then learned to reap their benefits by cooperating with them.

To reap the gifts of building assets, insights, infrastructure, expansion, experience, or a lifestyle that we want during expansion, we need diversity. Because this cycle delves into the unknown, our possibilities need to be open. With great awareness, we have to explore possible avenues accessible to us and knock on doors that beckon. We watch with great care for indicators in the environment, trying the new and exploring even the unlikely if indicated. Diverse approaches maximize our chances of achieving.

Like a tube torus, or a large donut folding outwards during the expansion period, the bottom, unseen, is folding inward. This means that even during the expression of passion as the dominant emotion, the emotion of joy lingers out of sight as a guiding force. When we knock on the doors before us and they reveal a possible future, the next question is: "What will make my heart sing?" In this way, our inner joy helps guide us in our choices.

We must be willing to act and take risks when guided. To think we can either control or predict the future closes the doors of possibility. Sometimes we have to be courageous in trying something, but with great awareness as to the consequences of our actions. When we act, it must always benefit indwelling life.

If the cycle of expansion with its diversification can be equated to throwing mud on the wall to see what will stick, the contraction cycle's gift of de-structuring cleans up the mud that didn't. It is during the contraction cycle when joy is dominant that the joyless pieces of our life are seen for what they are and discarded. Saying 'no' to the irrelevant pieces of our lives, allows room for a bigger 'yes' to possibilities even greater than before.

An example of successful contraction can be seen in the rise and decline of the British Empire. Its expansion included incorporating many diverse cultures into a sprawling umbrella state. Had it clung tenaciously to its territories, it would eventually have been conquered. It was spread too thin and its many families who were displaced around the world were eager to return to their roots. Instead of waiting for forced change, Britain relinquished many territories but kept those that contributed and were manageable and wished to remain part of the commonwealth. When war came to its island shores, it had the benefit of an expanded infrastructure, a strong foundation of industry, many allies and a wealth of experience from its period of expansion-related conflicts. In addition, its soldiers weren't battle weary from fighting too many territorial wars.

The periods of alternating activity and contemplation are mirrored in nature by the cycles of day and night and summer and winter. The tiger pauses before he pounces. Fields lie fallow before they sprout. Life goes from complexity and diversity to simplicity and back again in ever expanding cycles. If we bring our lives into harmony with these rhythms more ancient than the cosmos, we must prosper in every conceivable way.

Impeccability vs. Integrity

Integrity, as the word is generally used, refers to a standard of conduct that is universal and can be applied to everyone. Impeccability means you are acting upon the highest truth or perception available to you.

Because we are exploring the unknown through our actions on a moment by moment basis, our perception and interpretation of truth (the way the purpose of the Infinite should unfold) is developing accordingly. Today's level of perception is not yesterday's and our impeccability will be based on the various levels of changing perception.

Often we berate ourselves because of past actions we view as mistakes. This is one of the primary causes of guilt. Guilt causes us to want to avoid it through selective perception, which creates internal dialogue and traps us in the mind. The guilt is especially strong if others suffered from our blindness. But everyone enters our lives at the exact right time to receive from us the gifts and mirrors we bring to help them solve that portion of the mystery they contracted with the Infinite to solve.

On the other hand, to act un-impeccably is to be un-integrated in that the perception does not match the action. This could stem from either deliberately acting contrary to what we know to be the highest choice or not being truthful with ourselves about where the action originated.

Universal integrity, on the other hand, is supportive of indwelling life. It is the source of actions that do not warp the web of the inter-connectedness of life. It is the ultimate standard by which the conduct of man can be measured, no matter what belief systems or creeds he espouses. It is the highest form of honor a human being can live by. It leaves no karma and excludes none from its benefit for it holds the greater vision of the oneness of life. All benefit equally from the actions of one who walks in universal integrity.

One who walks in impeccability, living always his or her highest truth, must progress rapidly in unfolding their personal awareness. The perception of such a person increases as the horizon forever recedes. At first, occasional flashes of universal integrity might occur, but eventually it will become a way of life. For impeccability has to lead to the impersonal life where the greater good is always the first consideration, until finally the ego is stilled and God-consciousness is reached.

What is Karma?

When we examine the four building blocks of the Infinite and its Creation–time, space, energy, matter–they can be imagined as a river. The banks and shape of the river are space; the movement of the water is time; the force of the water is energy and the water itself is matter.

The river is the unfolding purpose of the Infinite. The one certainty is that it will move. If there is an obstacle, the river will either flow around it or increase its force until it breaks through. As life spirals forward it carries unresolved mysteries (unexplored insights) with it until we turn them into light.

These unyielded insights are karma. Individual insights unresolved from previous lifetimes are held as constrictions within the etheric, emotional and sometimes physical bodies of man, obstructing the flow of energy from our higher bodies. Dharma, or collective karma of a nation or planet, is held in the grid of the planet. Again it resembles a constriction. These constrictions create new opportunities to explore the unresolved issues and gain the unyielded insights through experience.

Even though we seem to be exploring our own issues in an autonomous way, the interconnectedness of life has us playing a larger role. We are like mountain climbers connected by a rope, ascending a steep mountain. If one of us is weighted down with baggage (karma that is not dealt with) our ascent will be slower and everyone around us will be impeded in their ability to progress.

In tracking our karma we need to look for recurring themes and knee-jerk reactions. What is most helpful is regression into past lives. The amazing pattern of selflessness we will find as we trace our interaction back through lifetimes with those with whom we have experienced the greatest intensity of emotions, is able to remove the deepest grief. The answer to dissolving pain has always been perception. In this case we will discover with what dedication we have volunteered to be a mirror for one another and how committed we have always been to the evolution of awareness; that every act we have taken has had its source in divine love.

CHAPTER SIX

SETTING HUMANITY FREE

Why Prayers Aren't Answered

Human beings have felt very abandoned as they have bargained and pleaded and tried to continue to have faith in whatever form of god they have prayed to throughout the ages of human existence. Where are the answers to our prayers? Why does God not respond when we sincerely try to do our part?

Some have steadfastly maintained their belief in a God who rewards good with good and withholds or punishes when they are not good. After all, they have been told by their churches that if they cannot hear the voice of God or their prayers are not answered, there is something 'wrong' on their end. This has left the human race, which knows deep within that life should not have to be this hard, with an unbelievably large reservoir of guilt and shame.

This guilt is passed on from generation to generation, exacerbated by the teachings of most primary religions that flesh is an unworthy and unholy vehicle for the spirit. How can one embrace life joyously when housed in a 'sinful' or unworthy body? A joyless life is simply a slow death and thus instead of embracing life, much of humanity embraces death. This manifests self-defeating circumstances and a life filled with failure. Meanwhile, grief–the desire to change–prods and prods us into better perception and understanding.

This vicious cycle of guilt, shame, abandonment and grief in which mankind has been immersed, is so painful that one of two things happen: either they live in their heads, suppressing by their selective perception their feelings of anguish; or they live hedonistically. Either way, their lives are so shallow that they become more and more fruitless in yielding insights. The pain level has to increase because the very reason for existence (to evolve awareness) is ignored through such a life and the life-spirals of awareness become smaller and smaller. As the pain increases, they turn to drugs, alcohol, television, shopping, eating, working or even some form of religion or service which makes them feel 'worthy' again.

Some hide their pain at 'being abandoned by God' in rage, living destructively as though taunting God. "If you're not there for me, there's no point in being good." Others, having a small fragment of what they perceive as truth, cling to it for dear life in this scenario of uncertainty. They try to convert everyone along the way to their 'only' truth with a great deal of dogmatic fervor.

What are the perceptions that life is prodding us to get about what prayer really is and how we can be masters of our own fate?

Perceptions Regarding Prayer:

- As noted above, we have been praying to God the Father, God the I AM or God the Creator. This is the equivalent of the physical body asking the mental or emotional body to make it better when the unresolved portions of the mental and emotional bodies are the very reason for the physical discomfort. In other words, we expect the patient to be the doctor.

  Solution:

  Communicating with our own highest self that holds the blueprint for our various lifetimes is far more conducive to realigning with our purpose. However, if we wish to impose our will on the path we are walking in a way that does not serve that purpose, assistance will be withheld. If our prayers are for the planet, which is part of the physical body of God, then directing our petition to the three higher bodies of the Infinite, the spiritual emotional, the spiritual mental and the spirit body (the true Mother of the I AM) is the most direct channel. If the concept of the Mother of God is too vast for us, the higher self can guide us but will not in any way change the original blueprint.

- Prayers may take longer to answer than we realize because the very nature of the word 'density' denotes a more complex relationship between time and space. This means the process by which the purpose of the Infinite unfolds is slowed, and there is a much longer gap between cause and effect. The personality who left my body on December 16, 2000 did so to diminish the pressure (suffering) on the denser levels of existence. But like a balloon that has received a pinhole in its wall, lessening the internal pressure, it still has to deflate gradually. So too, the release of suffering in answer to prayer takes time. As we have already seen, suffering precedes and prompts perception.

Somehow the unfolding of humankind's awareness will be less painful as a result of our prayers even though that process may take place over thousands or even millions of years.

Solution:

If we change our focus from form to indwelling life, we become free from expectations as to outcome or timing. If we do that, suffering is not the real tragedy but failing to use the priceless opportunity of learning information never accessed before and which we have contracted to learn. Having come to the only place in the cosmos where new insights can be obtained and then failing to learn them, places the burden on others who now have a double load to cope with.

The one who embraces challenge as the only way to gain this new knowledge has nothing to pray for. To remove one's challenges is to remove one's growth. The only option left is surrender to life with the utmost awareness. This dramatically decreases the level of pain required to prod change. Life becomes a fluid cooperative dance between the lightseeker and his higher self.

• We feel we cannot receive and hear guidance from higher realms. In some instances we may even feel as though our suffering is unfair since it comes to prod us into change when that would not be necessary if God would just tell us what to do. After all, is it not our obedience or the relinquishing of our will that God wants?

Solution:

God, in whatever form perceived, is light. Light is the known. We are exploring the unknown. If it is only obedience God wants, all growth would stop since it would always stay within the pool of the known. Let us look at it from a different angle. The Infinite has the tools to deal only with the known.

That is why the Infinite needs us: we deal with the unknown by feeling the indwelling life within it. Through feeling, we access the truth behind appearances. So the Infinite does not just need obedience, but our diligence as explorers of consciousness in learning the things the Infinite does not yet know. Relinquishing our will to the larger purpose of our being is inclusiveness. We do not ask for ease but for impeccability of conduct. We ask only for the clarity to see the highest choice each step of the way.

But how do we get this clarity if we cannot hear?

"... it does not speak to you with words to be heard by your ears, it is a voice to be felt, a vibration as sweet and unmistakable as the music of the Spheres."[11]

The two main reasons for our inability to hear are the roaring thunder of the internal dialog in our heads and the dulling of our ability to receive these delicate and refined vibrations because of the negative emotions caused by our incorrect perceptions. Through diligent recapitulation, filling our hearts with love, praise and gratitude and practice, we no longer need to "...strain or make an effort, just sit in silence and let coherent Light play across the weary brain cells of your surface mind... trust, obey and love it and your receptivity will increase."

But even as the highest wisdom guides you, know that because you are blazing a trail into the unknown there are simply places where you have to walk, sometimes with faltering steps, through uncharted territory where no guidance other than your sense of what is life-enhancing exists. You can do it with impeccability as a shield and truth as your armor. You have come here just for this purpose with the keen sword of awareness to cut a broad swath from the darkness and turn it into light.

11 From *The Door of Everything*, Ruby Nelson, pg. 154

• There is a general misconception of what prayer is. Prayer is that which through intent manipulates or affects the nature of reality. Thoughts fall into the reservoir of the heart and, combined with emotion, act upon the substance of things hoped for; those infinitesimally small cosmic rays that become atoms to form matter. Therefore, thoughts plus feelings create our life's circumstances. What then is our most predominant prayer, the few hastily uttered words at night or the thoughts that occupy our minds all day?

The ability of human beings to create their own reality is not an accident–we are the microcosm of the macrocosm with the same creative ability as the Infinite that used thought plus emotion to create us. But the violence and other negativities of the entertainment world in which our children grow up, load the mind with negative thoughts and create a negative environment.

As we allow fear (often externally imposed) to get a foothold in our emotions, the negative thoughts and emotions create a negative world. We have done this innocently, not realizing we are as powerful as we are. The true power of man has been deliberately obscured by those who have played the light-detractors because of how much hinges on us. Few beings in the cosmos have been aware of just how vast a role we play and will be playing. Even the light-promoters had only an inkling of the power inherent in man.

Solution:

Because of the ability to warp the web of interconnectedness that includes all life and create karma, warriors of light stalk their minds endlessly. They strive to fill their minds with only the most beautiful thoughts possible for this is their prayer. They create their reality consciously, reverently and with joy.

What a tragedy that few have understood the great gift of self-determination that has been bestowed on humankind, wallowing instead in the mire of self-pity and resentment that life is not better than it is and that some omnipotent, far off God does not heed their prayers to eliminate the negative results of their own making. We may be the child in terms of being the created offspring of the Infinite, but we have been endowed with all we need to grow up and create the beautiful world we pray for.

The Core Grief of Humanity

As we deal with our challenges, they peel away like layers of an onion until only the core is left. There is usually a personal core issue as well as a racial core issue. The core personal issue is determined by our contract with the Infinite as to what portion of the mystery we will solve and the unresolved pieces, or karma, resulting from the experiences we have designed in order to learn our insights. As we look at the racial issue of humankind, we find that each individual is tackling it in a slightly different way and from a unique perspective.

In the case of humanity, these issues have been the cause of massive destruction that has seemed on the surface to be impossible to prevent. This feeling of being a sitting duck waiting for the next catastrophe to hit has created a feeling of deep shame at our powerlessness, rage at feeling trapped in the victim role, frustration at being unable to protect our loved ones and, ultimately, a deep grief as the result of our vulnerability. We feel unsafe, so we become controlling, but this very resistance to life makes us vulnerable to death and disease.

Because most feel life could be swept away at any time, they live hedonistically as though there is no tomorrow. They live shallowly because the reservoir of pain inside is so deep that they fear any more will drown them. They stay in mental activity, shunning the silence by engaging in video games, TV or anything that will keep them there. That in turn makes them even less aware of signals indicating that they may need to prepare and protect themselves. So they once again get taken by surprise.

Surprise drains energy. Energy is needed for consciousness. When the shock of a catastrophe drains enough energy, an entire race or civilization could fall in consciousness. This is precisely what has happened to man.

Having come from the future, the souls who incarnated into the bodies of humankind (a 'new' creation and a synthesis of all the parent races) fell in consciousness due to the shock of the catastrophic devastation that had taken place. Once here, disasters continued to be experienced for, as in the future, black magic introduced by hostile star beings was practiced, disturbing the interconnectedness of life and wrecking havoc. The oral history of the Toltecs speaks of four great cataclysms that have caused a descension of humankind.

The first major cataclysm reported in Toltec oral history occurred 1,000,000 years ago when the surface of the earth changed dramatically and Atlantis rose to become a significant landmass.

A second cataclysm resulted from a series of volcanic eruptions that took place 800,000 years ago and sunk most of what had been the vast empire of Lemuria. Atlantis was broken up into a multitude of islands. The third catastrophe occurred 200,000 years ago, revealing land in northern Asia that had been submerged up to this point. The oral traditions say the greatest calamity of all was the thrusting up of the Himalayas where a very densely populated fertile plain had existed.

Around 75,000 years ago, a tilt in the earth's axis caused a wall of water, ice and debris to push southward over the Americas and the remnants of Atlantis. Another wall of water without ice rushed northward over Asia. The result was the emergence of the Americas of today, most of Asia becoming visible except for a large central sea, and the uplifting of much of Africa. Australia had reached its present size and Atlantis was about two-thirds the size of Australia. Atlantis and what was left of Gondwanaland sank in a single day 9,564 years before the crucifixion of Christ.

This brief overview shows the burden of grief held in the memory of mankind. The mentality of post-traumatic stress that will cause us to even destroy our own habitat is a result of that grief. In spite of the devastation and its memories, however, the ancient wisdom has survived lustrous and bright. Sometimes openly, sometimes invisibly, a little band of Toltecs and their descendants have endeavored to preserve the remaining fragments of that knowledge. This is all that remains of the wisdom of the Motherland.

What, then, is the answer to our inability to prevent such disasters? Firstly, being able to develop the right information-gathering tools to use for the known and the unknown; secondly, to be able to access the other realities available to man. This enables us to walk in and out of realities as someone would walk from one room to another. This has been the case with some entire ancient tribes. When threatened, they left one reality for another, not victims but masters of their own destiny.

Zero Point–The Key to Sovereignty

Loss of sovereignty is proportionate to surrendering to control from outside sources. Control can come into our lives like a thief in the night, stealthily stealing our freedom of choice, or it can come with teeth bared in a display of overwhelming force.

Each different age group has its own particular vulnerability to allowing the ideas of others to be imprinted on the psyche, obscuring the promptings of destiny.

Small children and the more enlightened have one thing in common; they only know that they don't know. The more conscious we become, the more apparent it is that we are living in a world of mirrors: that form is not real and that that which is cannot be accessed by the mind and the five senses. When those who have such certainty about the way things are give us the answers, we fail to see that all they have is a sliver of mirror and assume they know.

Small children and those who have left ego-identification behind are in God-consciousness. In the case of young children, this condition lasts about the first nine months of life. For those in God-consciousness the inner world is so expanded that the illusory boundaries of form have little meaning. Therefore, they only allow. This makes them completely open to the control of another. While their spirits are free, the form side of life can yet be controlled.

In pre-teen years, children are innately connected with their sub-personalities. Their inner warrior fights for what it wants, whether it's a toy or not having to go to bed. It is a fact that the inner nurturer takes care of the child and is at one with the inner child and its needs. For example, the child asks for what it wants; the biggest cookie, the softest place on the couch. The inner sage guidance reveals who is a 'bad' person and even though the mother may try to get the child to be polite to that person, he will say, "I don't like him".

The unbroken family unit further mirrors to the child these inner pieces. The mother takes care of the child's needs, the father protects the child and the grandparent has the time to share wisdom through stories of their own life.

But during these pre-teen childhood years, the child identifies with the mirrors of its sub-personalities–its family. "When I grow up I want to be just like Dad" is often spoken by a young boy as he pretends to hunt or fish or be a soldier like his father. Little girls can be heard speaking to their dolls in the same tone their mother uses in speaking to them. And so slowly but surely the social conditioning of the family starts to determine the way the child sees him or herself and the world. This conditioning will control him, to one degree or another, the rest of his life unless he actively throws it off.

As the child enters the teenage years, he steps out of identifying with his family members and tries to find his own identity. Because humanity as a whole has not understood the value of the sub-personalities, the teenager is often encouraged to abandon them, causing intense pain of alienation from his inner pieces.

The inner child is shunned as not belonging in the tentative new identity of emerging adulthood. The inner child becomes disconnected and so the nurturer indulges the emerging adult which makes the teenager very egocentric. The result is that teenagers are wholly self-centered through most of their teenage years.

Because the warrior's job is to protect the sovereignty of the individual by guarding its borders, the greater the parental control over childhood, the more the teenager rebels against parental authority. Often they do not understand their own rebellion and feel guilt and confusion in addition to the pain of alienation. In this turmoil the gently guiding voice of the inner sage goes unheard.

The result of this inner identity crisis is that the teenager seeks his identity externally. The media capitalizes on this by marketing certain images as desirable. The teenager, lost and cut off from inner and parental guidance, now is able to be controlled into seeking identity through material things such as possessions, brand names and so forth. Peer groups now become a further source of not only identity but approval. The child that is raised with more disapproval than praise is particularly vulnerable to control by a peer group.

In our twenties as we step into adulthood, we find the overwhelming control of government, institutions and other systems eroding the illusion that we have the freedom to shape our world and be who we want to be. Instead, the demands of the world now shape us. There are bills to pay, job applications, taxes, the requirements of employers.

The idea of a free human being seems to be a myth as we find ourselves controlled by the demands of material life, the bondage of social conditioning and, in the event of a painful childhood, the hold past pain has on us. Where then can the concept of freedom be found and lived in physicality? The answer lies in that place of complete silence; the place where time does not exist: Zero point.

For those who live in the constant clamor of their minds, it is hard to imagine an existence where silence is the prevailing state of the mind. This silence within is the hallmark of one who no longer identifies with ego and form, but instead has become one with his true identity; a being as vast as the cosmos having a human experience.

During the first three phases of God-Consciousness (the emptiness, the fullness or bliss and the stage of re-entry into human experience) we interrupt our silence only to relate to another. Eventually, as we enter into the final stage of the evolution of human awareness, the Immortal Master, our speech and our writing have no conscious thoughts behind them. Even when we relate to others we remain in the silence. We have entered what can be called the null, or zero point.

Within this stage we resonate only with that which is real, indwelling life. The world of form can be seen for the illusion it is and has no further hold on us. No earthly ambitions or temptations can control us. Even the greatest controller of all, death, must yield to us for we have ceased to oppose life.

Thoughts arise as an opposition to life. The mind's internal dialog is the result of selective perception in order to avoid looking at certain aspects of our lives. It is within the ability of every truth seeker to silence this dialog to such an extent that something as simple as a peak spiritual experience or a key insight can transfigure us in a moment into God-consciousness.

We are vulnerable during the first two stages of God-consciousness to the violation of our boundaries. But then we move into the human experience again because we realize that our most valuable contribution to the Infinite is insight gained through experience. Once again, we protect the 'boundaries' of the character we play on the stage of life, not because we believe the boundaries to be real, but that others may learn.

To achieve this inner freedom and sovereignty, this place of timelessness and silence, the internal dialog that maintains the barriers within our mind that let us see only what we expect to see has to be silenced. This requires disciplined perseverance in extracting from past experience its unyielded insights.

We start with present events that pull our strings and track any similar events in our past until we identify the underlying issues we are trying to solve through our experiences. We then ascertain what the insights and the gifts of the event are. Setting aside a half an hour each night to retrieve the insights of the day is a good beginning. Larger issues can then be tackled them during a designated block of time once a week.

As we practice watching with great care whether our responses are programmed or guided by inner wisdom, and strive to gain the insights that lie hidden within the pain of the past, our mind becomes more and more still. Less energy is wasted in rambling thoughts. Then suddenly, when a critical mass of personal power has been accrued, we find ourselves making that leap to freedom. No longer can we be governed by fear, for to fear another is to fear ourself. Though initially our forms may yet be destroyed, our spirits are finally free. As we journey through the stages of God-consciousness into those of Ascended Mastery, we eventually become free even from mortal boundaries and death.[12]

What is Zero Point?

What is that place of no-time that lies within a human heart? It is the place where masters live in order to compress time. For those in the environment of such a one, it may seem as though the master has a whirlwind of chaos around him or her. But chaos to one with limited vision is simply a higher order to another.

Most of us may have experienced compressed time on one occasion or another. For example, when involved in a car accident, the moments before impact seen like an eternity in which we assess the safety of everyone in the vehicle, decide where to expect the impact and much more. This slowing of time is what we live in when we always compress time. To a spectator, it may seem as though everything is proceeding at its usual pace; the slowing of time is an internal experience only.

Living in that place of no-time is much more than just a useful technique to separate for careful inspection the threads of the weaving of life. It is the place where thoughts still and within that stillness all things become possible. It is the implied culmination of meditational practices where meditation becomes a way of life. It is the place where neither the burdens of yesterday nor the cares

12 See The *Path to Freedom Volume I* on gaining insight from experience

of tomorrow weigh us down. It is truly the holy of holies where age ceases and the magic of childhood returns for it is also the place of innocence.

Zero point cannot be achieved through reason or logic but is the result of our full attention to the now. It is a place of heightened awareness, unencumbered by self-reflection. It is the peephole into eternity where all things become equally unimportant in view of the larger perspective.

The unfolding cosmos like a huge rolling tube torus is similar to that created by the human heart. An opened human heart forms a tube torus of energy which expands as our compassion becomes more inclusive. Thoughts that are not stilled interrupt this unfolding field of heart energy by closing down the heart and pulling us out of the moment.

When we enter into the moment with full awareness as though no other moment exists, the tube torus of our heart aligns with the tube torus of the cosmos. We become centered to the cosmic zero point. It is as though we have entered into the heart of God where we are able to contribute most effectively to the unfoldment of the cosmos by using the insights gained through our experience.

The Tools of Discernment

Cultivation of tools that access both the known and the unknown is essential. People who are very good at analyzing, or dealing with the known, often unsuccessfully rely on it to tackle the unknown. Those who are good at feeling, which is a tool for the unknown, are often unable to analyze their feelings, making them unsure of how to act in response to them. Each person must cultivate all four tools of discernment in order to raise awareness and access as much of reality as possible.

The Four Practices

There are four practices (See Figure 24, Tools of Discernment Within the Bands of Compassion & Figure 25, Practices to Develop the Tools) that, when incorporated into everyday life, yield the four tools of discernment.

1. **Shedding Our Worldviews**. Discarding the social conditioning that keeps us in bondage requires that we painstakingly track the motive behind every action. In this way, moment by moment, we find and get rid of the areas of our lives that are a programmed response. Additionally, we trace the origins of every reaction until we find the original event that triggered it. This has to be re-capitulated (see #2) to yield the insights that release its power. The unenlightened blindly react, but the one who has brought clarity to all areas of his or her life, masterfully responds from a place of stillness and with original thought.

2. **Recapitulation.** We go through the events that still 'pull our strings' to find the lesson, the contract, and identify our role. We take a careful look at what the mirrors show: Is it something we are or something we have yet to develop? Is it something we judge or something we have given away? What is the gift? We see through past life regressions[13] what part of the bigger puzzle we are trying to solve. As we re-capitulate more and more of our life, one day we find we have achieved a miracle; the inner dialog of the mind has made way for silence and within the silence, all things are possible.[14]

3. **Eliminating** our personal identity. We become trapped by labels given by others and those we give ourselves. These boxes in our minds create blind spots and obscure pure feeling. We elim-

---

13 More fully discussed in *A Life of Miracles*
14 In-depth teaching is available on recordings of *The Path to Freedom Volume I*

Tools of Discernment within the Bands of Compassion

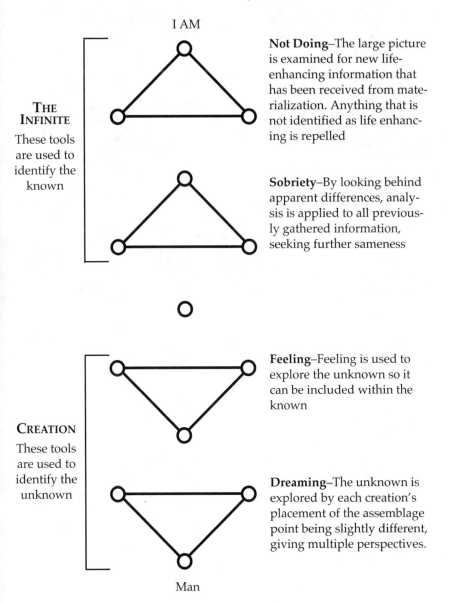

I AM

THE INFINITE

These tools are used to identify the known

Not Doing–The large picture is examined for new life-enhancing information that has been received from materialization. Anything that is not identified as life enhancing is repelled

Sobriety–By looking behind apparent differences, analysis is applied to all previously gathered information, seeking further sameness

CREATION

These tools are used to identify the unknown

Feeling–Feeling is used to explore the unknown so it can be included within the known

Dreaming–The unknown is explored by each creation's placement of the assemblage point being slightly different, giving multiple perspectives.

Man

The Four Great Bands of Compassion can also be called trinities since each contains a positive, negative and neutral component.

(Figure 24)

Practices to Develop the Tools

Eliminating World Views
Discarding belief systems and
eliminating social conditioning

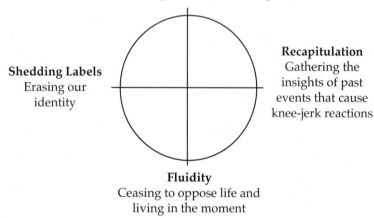

Shedding Labels
Erasing our
identity

Recapitulation
Gathering the
insights of past
events that cause
knee-jerk reactions

Fluidity
Ceasing to oppose life and
living in the moment

Tools of Discernment

Not-Doing
The art of observing the overall
scene from a large perspective

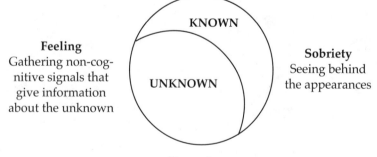

KNOWN

UNKNOWN

Feeling
Gathering non-cog-
nitive signals that
give information
about the unknown

Sobriety
Seeing behind
the appearances

Dreaming
The art of altering perception through
the movement of the assemblage point

(Figure 25)

inate them by watching which of our roles we believe to be our
identity.

4. **Cultivating fluidity.** We do this by ceasing to oppose life. We
cultivate an attitude that flows with the changes that come our
way. We get rid of rigid attitudes by stretching our comfort zone
a little more each day and living with complete focus on the
moment. The attitude of fluidity travels lightly through life,
leaving the burdens of moments gone by behind and keeping
only the insights. Fluidity cooperates fully with life, unencumbered by the weight of self-reflection; able to change directions
at a moment's notice.

The Four Principal Tools of Discernment

1. **Dreaming** is the result of a sustained movement of the assemblage point and is used to discern the unknown. During sleep it
moves to a certain position and the dream symbols that result
are a means of interpreting the unknown. During meditation we
also maintain a slight shift and answers about the unknown sub-
tly present themselves. But the true power behind this amazing
tool only manifests once we have silenced the dialog within our
minds. At this level of awareness, moving in and out of altered
perception becomes second nature.

2. **Feeling.** It is imperative that the following two tools be used as
objectively as possible and this and the previous tool as subjec-
tively as possible. The unknown is accessed by this tool through
non-cognitive impressions about indwelling life. To avoid
becoming trapped in the world of mirrors or appearances, our
first assessment of anything is done with dreaming. Further
impressions are then gathered with this tool. No longer having
any labels to uphold, we are not invested in being right, only in
learning the purpose of indwelling life as it unfolds before us.

We notice, therefore, any nuance we can pick up through our feelings. Feeling as a tool to access the unknown is reliable once all personal identity is gone.

3. **Sobriety.** This is the ability to see behind the appearances and beyond the obvious. Sobriety is a tool for the known. We know that the face value of anything belies that which is really going on; that which is the intended purpose of indwelling life hiding within form. The careful analysis that is part of sobriety includes looking at any symbols in the environment that reflect the true meaning of the event, and analyzing the non-cognitive information of the previous two tools. When using sobriety to obtain an answer such as what choice to make about a set of known facts, we pose the question clearly and then observe what stands out on the horizon of our experience. Perhaps we almost stepped on a dead snake. We realize the snake represents wisdom and we were about to step where wisdom is dead. Sobriety is a tool for the known.

4. **Not-Doing or Eagle Vision**, We use this tool to assess the known, much like the eagle does as it soars high above the valley, looking at every detail but also seeing the big picture. It helps us step outside of events so we can be completely objective in our assessment. This also ensures that not even in the heat of battle do we lose the perspective that ensures we act impeccably. From the eagle's perspective all are equally important.

Not-doing is like interlocking the detailed analysis obtained from the previous tool, sobriety, to form a partially completed puzzle and then deducing the rest of the picture. Men and women of vision that have mastered this art have been the ones that have been accomplishing ahead of the times in which they have lived.

Not only do these four tools help us to be as aware as possible to avoid being taken by surprise, but they help us gain the insights that will silence the mind.

There are thirty-two different realities available to man; 10 accomplished by maintaining a full shift of the assemblage point and 22 the result of partial shifts. Within the silence of the mind lies the ability to accomplish these shifts and slip in and out of this reality. With enough personal power, you can even take others with you as did the ancient Inca or the Anasazi, for example.

Whether we use these tools for such deep mystical purposes as changing realities altogether, as a means of silencing the mind by gaining insights from experience, or to help us interpret reality, we will find they have set us free from the mirrors.

No more do we wait for catastrophe in helpless despair. No longer are we captive to the tyranny of unforeseen events. We have become free beings of the cosmos and after a life lived in discipline and joy, may just slip past the greatest tyrant of all–death.

Duty

The first and foremost duty and responsibility we undertook to fulfill is that contract we made with the Infinite at the dawn of Creation, as to what part of the mystery of beingness we will solve. As our higher selves design our experiences, this sacred task and duty is the determining factor for each and every life.

Not even the smallest particle of energy or experience is wasted; all things exist to evolve awareness. Lucifer's rage is used to facilitate the stepping down of light into matter. Even the blind spots we have that create karmic consequence are used as mirrors, not only for us to see, but also for others to experience mirrors of their destinies or contracts.

Our contracts with the Infinite, which we call our destinies, touch the destinies of others exactly the way pentagons touch each other to make a dodecahedron, like the surface of a soccer ball. There are usually five others that touch each person lifetime after lifetime. For instance, Jane might have as her duty the solving of how suffering can cause the enhancement of learning versus the loss of consciousness. Peter might be studying how the gap of perception between a victim and a perpetrator can be bridged. They may find they are incarnating together, mirroring various roles for each other lifetime after lifetime.

Our higher selves receive the big picture of why we are entering Creation (our destinies) from our highest selves (our individuation within the Creator) and know what we need to accomplish during our incarnations. The roles we are playing are designed to fulfill our contracts. To wish we had someone else's role is foolish beyond comprehension if we look at it from this perspective. We fight so hard at times against the opposition of our lives when every minute detail was designed by ourselves to maximize our chances of gaining those insights necessary for our destiny.

The misguided sense of duty that most people have is the result of believing the mirrors of life to be real. They give their alliances to belief systems that imprison man and bind progress in exchange for the feeling of belonging that temporarily assuages the pain of alienation from their inner divinity.

When we live less than our highest truth, we also impede the growth of others in our soul family with whom we have been incarnating. When we accept the unacceptable or cover and compensate for the mistakes of others, this misguided sense of duty prevents them from growing, as well as ourselves.

In asking where our highest duty lies, the answer will always be the same: with that which promotes the evolution of indwelling life. Whether painful or pleasurable, this criterion allows us to fulfill at all times our highest calling.

The Bondage of Darkness

Distorted perception yields distorted emotion. When emotion is distorted from experience that has not yielded its insights, it distorts current perception in turn. Therefore, a downward spiral occurs that darkens higher vision to such an extent that even innate impulses become twisted.

Innate impulses, or the instinctual wisdom of man, receive their wisdom from the grid of the species. Each species has a geometric array of lines of light that gives it direction pertaining to the fulfillment of that specie's destiny. Think of it as the guidance system that should kick in when an individual loses his way. In the seven directions this part of the psyche is the direction of below. When an individual spirals downward in a vortex of confusion and illusion, the basic messages telling him how to be are also distorted.

The basic instinct of a human being speaks in gentle whisperings of a far, far greater destiny than meets the eye. It prods man into the knowledge that even a seemingly insignificant act could be the hinge upon which destiny swings. Such an impulse, seen through distortion, could cause the person to seek empowerment through the use of black magic. Black magic, the use of first-ring magic[15] for life-destructive purposes, does not require the accumulation of personal power through perception. As a consequence, it does not have accompanying insight to guide its use. It is a left-brain oriented skill that can be acquired to some degree by anyone with a teacher. A small act can cause great damage (how great depends on the skill level) and so the feeling of empowerment to

15 First-ring magic uses external techniques, whereas second-ring magic is the manipulation of reality through internal technology and by the power of intent.

271

impact life is felt by the black magician. It is a distorted and an upside-down perception of the destiny of man.

Any attempt to harm life or to exert our will upon the unfolding of destiny in this way distorts the web of life and creates karma for the practitioner. This brings more spells and curses directed back at the practitioner, further distorting his perception. A spell is, in many cases, a distorted cage of light placed around someone else.

The less black magicians can see, the less able they are to change until they are trapped in a web of their own making. Pain, striving to force them into change, becomes increasingly aggravated. To escape it, they move further and further into their minds, increasing their selective perception that prevents them from seeing how to reverse their downward spiral, reducing their ability to feel anything at all. They are then trapped, unable to receive guidance while accumulating increasingly painful karma.

The fate of black magicians and their downward spiral could as easily apply to any who commit inconceivably hostile acts against humanity and nature. Light promoters find perpetrators of all kinds in various lifetimes that leave them shattered or in shock. It is very difficult to understand that which is not within.

Rage is a natural result of suppressed light. It serves to break up decaying or stagnant patterns. Huge, uncontrollable rage could well be the last attempt by a perpetrator to break free from the ever-thickening prison bars of his own making. As long as he can feel, he can at least know he is alive and a faint glimmer of hope remains. But to the pure in heart, a wall of rage can be devastating. Why would we manifest such darkness in lives dedicated to reaching for the light?

Because we can see from a higher perspective and because we feel deep compassion for all life, we suffer their presence in our lives in order to gain understanding of what causes such a descent into darkness. The evolution of awareness requires certain experiences to explore certain portions of the Infinite's being. If we gain those insights for others, their painful experiences are not wasted and we gently and compassionately lift them off their treadmill. They now become free to more productively explore other portions of the mystery.

Karma is not punitive. It is merely blind spots begging for resolution through insight-yielding experience. By gaining insights on behalf of those struggling with darkness, we assist in removing their karma through grace. We become a savior to others in the truest sense of the word. In exchange, our own light increases.

When we finally expand our vision to such a degree that we can see these souls for what they truly are, gratitude floods our hearts and can lift us into ascension. If such a role had to be played to produce certain insights, these beleaguered ones have assumed the role of joyless descension out of a belief in the purpose of the Infinite. They have also done it so we did not have to. Perhaps for many lifetimes all we could see was the self-pity of our role as victim and they had to repeat their roles as perpetrators, trusting that we would eventually learn the lessons and raise them up again.

As the One expressing as the Many, we have come from love. Even as we look into the darkest places within Creation, all we ultimately find there is love.

Original Thinking– The Password to the Stars

In separation consciousness the most dominant form of awareness is Evolving Awareness. The evolution of awareness takes place through cycles of challenge that progress through the three distinct stages of transformation, transmutation and transfiguration. Learning opportunities are maximized during these cycles by the presence of a great deal of opposition and the repetitive nature of the cycles that make sure we learn by presenting the challenges again and again until we get their insights.

In God-consciousness the vast vision that comes as the gift of Inherent Awareness is experienced in its fullness. This awareness that originates within the Infinite travels outwards in a flat straight line that presents very few learning opportunities–the reason the Infinite formed Creation (where Evolving Awareness originates) to gather its insights. If someone in God-consciousness stays in the bliss, growth stops. The challenge is to re-enter the human condition and enact the cycles of experience while keeping the greater vision. This combining of Inherent and Evolving Awarenesses is essential for progress to the final stage of human evolution: Ascended Mastery.

Prior to entering God-consciousness all old programming is cleared out as the mind becomes silent. The challenge becomes that, having old ways of thinking erased, we not fill the resulting emptiness of mind with new prompts from our environment. There is the tendency for a master in God-consciousness to only allow; to permit outside influences to tell us how to act.

During the third phase of God-consciousness, it is essential that the master come to grips with the fact that those who are so eager to tell the master how to act can only see the mirrors, whereas the master now serves only indwelling life. If the master resists the temptation to allow others to run his life and once again establishes borders so that others may learn, he can progress to Ascended Mastery.

During Ascended Mastery the meaning of true genius becomes apparent as the master taps into the source of all knowledge: Original Awareness. Ascended Mastery is the last stage before we enter the god-kingdom, able to issue the command "Let there be light" and have it be so. As vehicles of the will of the Infinite we cannot receive directions from the mirrors in our environment but must open instead to the pure, steady flow of information from Source through Original Awareness; that arching form of awareness that produces true original thinking. Only when we allow pure original thinking to flood our being do we become co-creators with the Divine and take up the mantle of responsibility of one who has become the I am that I am.

Self-referring for approval, no longer engaging in the petty games of others in order to pacify those of lesser perception, the master becomes the crowning glory of the cosmos: a sovereign, self-sustaining being. The master's destiny can now come to full fruition as he takes his place as one of the wayshowers among the stars, a light until all life and a jewel in the crown of the Living God.

Closing

I have marveled at the revelations of the deep mysteries of creation as they have unfolded through the writing of this book. I am in awe at the perfection and infinite wisdom that govern all life. From the silence of Source this great light has been shed on the magnificent destiny and origins of man.

I am humbly grateful for these glimpses of eternity I have been permitted to experience and transcribe. Can such magnificent visions be shared? Will those led to search out this book feel their glory as I do? But then I feel you, those who will read these great truths, present around me as my pen flows across the paper and I know that it is you who are calling this information forth. It is you who refuse to accept the trite answers and the neatly packaged explanations made palatable by lofty sounding words. The purity of your spirits has demanded that the veil part and the truth of the cosmos be revealed.

Those sons and daughters of light who have come to earth to be the wayshowers, have come through time and space together; from the first moments of created life to meet upon this planet to turn the keys that will begin the journey home, back to the heart of God. I have been called forth for the specific task of touching the hearts of those who are pillars of the temple, who uphold humanity by the light of their presence now and in the future.

To you, my dearly beloved family, I dedicate this book. May your hearts recognize the many levels of light it imparts. May you and I pull forth even more light in the future that we may fill the earth with hope and peace and lay the path to a new tomorrow.

Prayer

Great God of light, in whom we dwell and have our being, fill our hearts with courage born of vision. And from this courage may we draw the strength to surrender to the unfolding of our lives, trusting where we cannot see, the perfection of thy plan.

To thee the glory forever and ever, Amen.